ASVAB MATH PRACTICE BOOK WITH 275 QUESTIONS

**5 Arithmetic Reasoning and
5 Mathematics Knowledge Practice Tests
with Math Review and Workbook
for the ASVAB Test and AFQT**

The drawings in this publication are for illustration purposes only. They are not drawn to an exact scale.

NOTE: The ASVAB and AFQT are registered trademarks of the United States Department of Defense, which is not affiliated with nor endorses this publication.

INFORMATION FOR EDUCATORS

If you are an educator, please respect copyright law. This book cannot be photocopied or reproduced electronically for use with students.

In order to use the book in a classroom, you should purchase a copy of the book for each of your students.

For those interested in purchasing sets of materials for classroom use, please contact us for information on bulk discounts. We may be contacted by filling in the "Contact Us" form at www.examsam.com.

TABLE OF CONTENTS

Arithmetic Reasoning Study Guide and Practice Tests

HOW TO USE THIS PUBLICATION

The arithmetic reasoning practice tests in this study guide contain questions of all of the types that you will see on the real ASVAB test.

Practice test 1 in this book is in "tutorial mode." To help you learn the concepts and formulas more quickly, the answers in practice test 1 are provided immediately after each question.

As you complete practice test 1, you should pay special attention to the tips highlighted in the special boxes. You should also study the explanations to the answers to practice test 1 especially carefully.

Although you will not see tips like this on the actual exam, these suggestions will help you improve your performance on each subsequent practice test in this publication.

Studying the tips and explanations in practice test 1 will help you obtain strategies to improve your performance on the other practice tests in this book.

Of course, these strategies will also help you do your best on the day of your actual ASVAB test.

After completing practice test 1, you should then try the other practice tests in the book. The answers to the questions in these practice tests are provided after each test.

Format of the ASVAB Arithmetic Reasoning Test

The ASVAB Arithmetic Reasoning Test contains thirty questions. ASVAB Arithmetic Reasoning questions may be placed into the following categories:

- Absolute Value
- Computations with Integers
- Estimation
- Exponent Laws
- Factorials
- Fractions
- Mixed Numbers
- Miles per Hour
- Order of Operations
- Perimeter
- Profit Calculations
- Price per Unit
- Percentages and Decimals
- Proportions
- Ratios
- Rate
- Scientific Notation
- Sequences and Prime Numbers
- Square Roots
- Statistics – Basic Probability, Arithmetic Mean, Median, and Mode
- Tax Calculations
- Units of Measurement

The practice tests in this study guide simulate the kinds of questions you will see on the actual ASVAB exam.

ASVAB MATH FORMULAS AT A GLANCE

COORDINATE GEOMETRY

- **Midpoints**

  Midpoint formula: $(x_1 + x_2) \div 2$, $(y_1 + y_2) \div 2$

- **Slope and slope-intercept**

  The slope formula is as follows: $m = \dfrac{y_2 - y_1}{x_2 - x_1}$

  The slope-intercept formula is: $y = mx + b$

  m is the slope and b is the y intercept.

- **Equation of a line**

  The equation of a line is: $ax + by = c$ or $0 = mx + b + c$

- **x and y intercepts**

  x intercept: point where line crosses the x axis. Represented by points $(x, 0)$

  y intercept: point where line crosses the y axis. Represented by points $(0, y)$.

PLANE AND SOLID GEOMETRY

Angle Laws

- *Triangles*: The sum of all three angles in any triangle must be equal to 180 degrees.
- *Parallel lines*: When two parallel lines are cut by a transversal, opposite angles will be equal in measure, and the corresponding angles will also be equal in measure.
- *Parallelograms*: A four-sided figure with parallel sides and two pairs of opposite angles.

Angles – Types of Angles

- *Congruent:* Angles that have the same measurement in degrees are called congruent angles.
- *Supplementary:* Two angles are supplementary if they add up to 180 degrees.
- *Complementary:* Two angles are complementary (sometimes called adjacent angles) if they add up to 90 degrees. This means that the two angles will form a right triangle.

Circles

- Area of a circle = $\pi \times r^2$ (radius squared)
- Circumference of a circle is = $\pi \times$ diameter
- Diameter = radius $\times$ 2

Boxes

- Box volume = base $\times$ width $\times$ height

Cones

- Cone volume = $(\pi \times radius^2 \times height) \div 3$

Cylinders

- Cylinder volume = $\pi \times radius^2 \times height$

Rectangles

- Area of a rectangle = length $\times$ width
- Perimeter of a rectangle = (length $\times$ 2) + (width $\times$ 2)

Squares

- Area of a square = length $\times$ width
- Perimeter of a square = (length $\times$ 2) + (width $\times$ 2)

Tubes

- Volume of a tube = $\pi \times radius^2 \times height$

Triangle Formulas

- Area of a triangle = (base × height) ÷ 2

- Hypotenuse length C = $\sqrt{A^2 + B^2}$

Triangle – Types of Triangles

- *Isosceles*: An isosceles triangle has two equal sides and two equal angles.

- *Equilateral*: An equilateral triangle has three equal sides and three equal angles. Equilateral triangles are also called congruent triangles.

PROBABILITY

- Probability is represented by the formula: $\frac{E}{S}$

- E = the event. This is the chance of the desired outcome.

- S = the "sample space". This is the number of items available in the total data set at the time of the event.

ASVAB ARITHMETIC REASONING - PRACTICE TEST 1
WITH MATH CONCEPT AND FORMULA REVIEW

1. Simplify: $| \, 3 - 6 \, |$
    A. -9
    B. -3
    C. 3
    D. 8

Absolute Value:

When you see numbers between lines like this $| -3 |$, you are being asked the absolute value. Absolute value is always a positive number. So, $|-2| = 2$

The correct answer is: C

Perform the operation on the numbers inside the absolute value symbols.

$| \, 3 - 6 \, | = | -3 |$

Then determine the absolute value.

$| -3 | = 3$

2. $-(-5) + 3 = ?$
    A. -8
    B. -2
    C. 2
    D. 8

Computations with Integers:

Integers are positive and negative whole numbers. Integers cannot have decimals, nor can they be mixed numbers. In other words, they can't contain fractions.

The correct answer is D.

One of the most important concepts to remember about integers is that two negative signs together make a positive number.

According to this concept, we know that $-(-5) = 5$

So, we can substitute this into the equation in order to solve it.

$-(-5) + 3 =$

$5 + 3 = 8$

3. Estimate the result of the following: $502 \div 49.1$
    A. 8
    B. 9
    C. 10
    D. 11

Estimation:

Estimation questions require you to determine the result of a problem without doing the full computation.

The correct answer is C.

STEP 1: When doing estimation problems, you need to round the numbers up or down.

As a rule of thumb, numbers less than 5 will be rounded down to the nearest 0 and numbers of 5 or more will be rounded up to the nearest 10.

Our problem was 502 ÷ 49.1

So, 502 is rounded down to 500 and 49.1 is rounded up to 50.

STEP 2: To estimate the result, we then perform the operation on the rounded figures.

$500 \div 50 = 10$

4. $11^5 \times 11^3 = ?$
A. 11^8
B. 11^{15}
C. 22^8
D. 121^8

Exponent Laws:

You will see questions that involve adding and subtracting exponents on your exam.

When the base numbers are the same and you need to multiply, you add the exponents. When the base numbers are the same and you need to divide, you subtract the exponents.

The correct answer is A.

The base number in this example is 11. So, we add the exponents: 5 + 3 = 8

We can prove the solution as follows:

$11^5 \times 11^3 =$

$11^{(5 + 3)} =$

11^8

5. $10^6 \div 10^4 = ?$
A. 10^{24}
B. 10^2
C. 20^{24}
D. 20^2

The correct answer is B.

The base number in this example is 10.

So, we subtract the exponents: 6 − 4 = 2

$10^6 \div 10^4 =$

$10^{(6 - 4)} =$

10^2

6.   What is the result of the following: 3!
A.   −3
B.   6
C.   3
D.   0

The correct answer is B.
Remember that you have to multiply the number provided, which is 3 in our problem, by every integer that is less than that number, which are 2 and 1.
3! = 3 × 2 × 1 = 6

7. What is $^1/_3$ × $^2/_3$?
    A. $^2/_3$
    B. $^2/_6$
    C. $^2/_9$
    D. $^1/_3$

The correct answer is C.
Multiply the numerators.
1 × 2 = 2
Then multiply the denominators.
3 × 3 = 9
These numbers form the new fraction: $^2/_9$

8. $\dfrac{1}{5} \div \dfrac{4}{7} = ?$

    A. $\dfrac{4}{20}$

    B. $\dfrac{7}{20}$

    C. $\dfrac{4}{35}$

    D. $\dfrac{5}{35}$

The correct answer is B.
Remember to invert the second fraction.

Inverting the fraction means that you put the denominator on the top and the numerator on the bottom.

Our problem was: $\dfrac{1}{5} \div \dfrac{4}{7} = ?$

So the second fraction $\dfrac{4}{7}$ becomes $\dfrac{7}{4}$ when inverted.

Now use the inverted fraction to solve the problem.

$\dfrac{1}{5} \div \dfrac{4}{7} =$

$\dfrac{1}{5} \times \dfrac{7}{4} = \dfrac{7}{20}$

9.   What is $\dfrac{1}{9} + \dfrac{9}{27}$?

A. $\dfrac{12}{27}$

B. $\dfrac{9}{27}$

C. $\dfrac{3}{27}$

D. $\dfrac{10}{36}$

Fractions – Finding the Lowest Common Denominator (LCD):
In some fraction problems, you will have to find the lowest common denominator.
In other words, before you add or subtract fractions, you have to change them so that the bottom numbers in each fraction are the same.
You do this by multiplying the numerator by the same number you use on the denominator for each fraction.

The correct answer is A.
Remember to multiply the numerator and denominator by the same number when you are converting to the LCD.

STEP 1: To find the LCD, you have to look at the factors for each denominator.
Factors are the numbers that equal a product when they are multiplied by each other.
So, the factors of 9 are:
1 × 9 = 9
3 × 3 = 9
The factors of 27 are:
1 × 27 = 27
3 × 9 = 27

STEP 2: Determine which factors are common to both denominators by comparing the lists of factors.

In this problem, the factors of 3 and 9 are common to the denominators of both fractions.

We can illustrate the common factors as shown. We saw that the factors of 9 were:

1 × **9** = 9

3 × 3 = 9

The factors of 27 were:

1 × 27 = 27

3 × **9** = 27

So, the numbers in bold above are the common factors.

STEP 3: Multiply the common factors to get the lowest common denominator.

The numbers that are in bold above are then used to calculate the lowest common denominator.

3 × 9 = 27

So, the lowest common denominator (LCD) for each fraction above is 27.

STEP 4: Convert the denominator of each fraction to the LCD.

You convert the fraction by referring to the factors from step 3.

Multiply the numerator and the denominator by the same factor.

Our problem was $\dfrac{1}{9} + \dfrac{9}{27} = ?$

So, we convert the first fraction as follows:

$$\dfrac{1}{9} \times \dfrac{3}{3} = \dfrac{3}{27}$$

We do not need to convert the second fraction of $\dfrac{9}{27}$ because it already has the LCD.

STEP 5: When both fractions have the same denominator, you can perform the operation to solve the problem.

$$\dfrac{1}{9} + \dfrac{9}{27} = \dfrac{3}{27} + \dfrac{9}{27} = \dfrac{12}{27}$$

10. Simplify: $\dfrac{12}{27}$

A. $\dfrac{1}{3}$

B. $\dfrac{3}{4}$

C. $\dfrac{3}{9}$

D. $\dfrac{4}{9}$

Fractions – Simplifying:

To simplify fractions, look to see what factors are common to both the numerator and denominator.

The correct answer is D.

STEP 1: Look at the factors of the numerator and denominator.
The factors of 12 are:
1 × 12 = 12
2 × 6 = 12
3 × 4 = 12
You will remember that the factors of 27 are:
1 × 27 = 27
3 × 9 = 27
So, we can see that the numerator and denominator have the common factor of 3.

STEP 2: Simplify the fraction by dividing the numerator and denominator by the common factor.

Our fraction in this problem is $\dfrac{12}{27}$.

So, simplify the numerator: 12 ÷ 3 = 4
Then simplify the denominator: 27 ÷ 3 = 9

STEP 3: Use the results from the previous step to form the new fraction.
The numerator from the previous step is 4.
The d0enominator is 9.

So, the new fraction is: $\dfrac{4}{9}$

11. $3\dfrac{1}{3} - 2\dfrac{1}{2} = ?$

   A. $\dfrac{1}{3}$

   B. $\dfrac{9}{3}$

   C. $\dfrac{5}{6}$

   D. $1\frac{1}{2}$

Mixed Numbers:

Mixed numbers are those that contain a whole number and a fraction. Convert the mixed numbers back to fractions first. Then find the lowest common denominator of the fractions in order to solve the problem.

The correct answer is C.

STEP 1: Convert the first mixed number to an integer plus a fraction.

$$3\tfrac{1}{3} = 3 + \frac{1}{3}$$

STEP 2: Then multiply the integer by a fraction whose numerator and denominator are the same as the denominator of the existing fraction.

$$3 + \frac{1}{3} =$$

$$\left(3 \times \frac{3}{3}\right) + \frac{1}{3} =$$

$$\frac{9}{3} + \frac{1}{3}$$

STEP 3: Add the two fractions to get your new fraction.

$$\frac{9}{3} + \frac{1}{3} = \frac{10}{3}$$

Then convert the second mixed number to a fraction, using the same steps that we have just completed for the first mixed number.

$$2\tfrac{1}{2} =$$

$$2 + \frac{1}{2} =$$

$$\left(2 \times \frac{2}{2}\right) + \frac{1}{2} =$$

$$\frac{4}{2} + \frac{1}{2} = \frac{5}{2}$$

Now that you have converted both mixed numbers to fractions, find the lowest common denominator and subtract to solve.

$$\frac{10}{3} - \frac{5}{2} =$$

$$\left(\frac{10}{3} \times \frac{2}{2}\right) - \left(\frac{5}{2} \times \frac{3}{3}\right) =$$

$$\frac{20}{6} - \frac{15}{6} = \frac{5}{6}$$

12. Sam is driving a truck at 70 miles per hour. At 10:30 am, he sees this sign:

Brownsville	**35 miles**
Dunnstun	**70 miles**
Farnam	**140 miles**
Georgetown	**210 miles**

After Sam sees the sign, he continues to drive at the same speed. At 11:00 am, how far will he be from Farnam?

A. He will be in Farnam.
B. He will be 35 miles from Farnam.
C. He will be 70 miles from Farnam.
D. He will be 105 miles from Farnam.

Miles per Hour:

To calculate miles per hour, divide the distance traveled in miles by the time spent traveling. On the other hand, to get the time spent traveling, multiply the miles per hour by the time.

The correct answer is D.

Sam is driving at 70 miles per hour, and at 10:30 am he is 140 miles from Farnam.

STEP 1: We need to find out how far he will be from Farnam at 11:00 am, so we need to work out how far he will travel in 30 minutes.

STEP 2: If Sam is traveling at 70 miles an hour, then he travels 35 minutes in half an hour.

70 miles in one hour × $\frac{1}{2}$ hour = 35 miles

STEP 3: If he was 140 miles from Farnam at 10:30 am, he will be 105 miles from Farnam at 11:00 am.

140 − 35 = 105 miles

13. $-6 \times 3 - 4 \div 2 = ?$
A. −20
B. −18
C. −2
D.   4

PEMDAS – Order of Operations:

The phrase "order of operations" means that you need to know which mathematical operation to do first when you are faced with longer problems.

"PEMDAS" means that you have to do the mathematical operations in this order:

First: Do operations inside **P**arentheses

Second: Do operations with **E**xponents

Third: Perform **M**ultiplication and **D**ivision (from left to right)

Last: Do **A**ddition and **S**ubtraction (from left to right)

The correct answer is A.

There are no parentheses or exponents in this problem, so we need to direct our attention to the multiplication and division first.

When you see a problem like this one, you need to do the multiplication and division from left to right.

This means that you take the number to the left of the multiplication or division symbol and multiply or divide that number on the left by the number on the right of the symbol.

So, in our problem we need to multiply −6 by 3 and then divide 4 by 2.

You can see the order of operations more clearly if you put in parentheses to group the numbers together.

$-6 \times 3 - 4 \div 2 =$

$(-6 \times 3) - (4 \div 2) =$

$-18 - 2 = -20$

11

14. $$\dfrac{5 \times (7-4)^2 + 3 \times 8}{5 - 6 \div (4-1)} = ?$$

    A. −23

    B. 23

    C. $\dfrac{23}{\frac{1}{3}}$

    D. 128

PEMDAS – Order of Operations:

Some students prefer to remember the order or operations by using the memorable phrase:

Please Excuse My Dear Aunt Sally

The correct answer is B.

For this type of problem, do the operations inside the **parentheses** first.

$$\dfrac{5 \times (7-4)^2 + 3 \times 8}{5 - 6 \div (4-1)} =$$

$$\dfrac{5 \times (3)^2 + 3 \times 8}{5 - 6 \div 3}$$

Then do the operation on the **exponent**.

$$\dfrac{5 \times (3)^2 + 3 \times 8}{5 - 6 \div 3} =$$

$$\dfrac{5 \times (3 \times 3) + 3 \times 8}{5 - 6 \div 3}$$

$$\dfrac{5 \times 9 + 3 \times 8}{5 - 6 \div 3}$$

Then do the **multiplication** and **division**.

$$\dfrac{5 \times 9 + 3 \times 8}{5 - 6 \div 3} =$$

$$\dfrac{(5 \times 9) + (3 \times 8)}{5 - (6 \div 3)} =$$

$$\dfrac{45 + 24}{5 - 2}$$

Then do the **addition** and **subtraction**.

$$\dfrac{45 + 24}{5 - 2} = \dfrac{69}{3}$$

In this case, we can then simplify the fraction since both the numerator and denominator are divisible by 3.

$$\frac{69}{3} = 69 \div 3 = 23$$

15. Farmer Brown has a field in which cows craze. He is going to buy fence panels to put up a fence along one side of the field. Each panel is 8 feet 6 inches long. He needs 11 panels to cover the entire side of the field. How long is the field?
     A. 60 feet 6 inches
     B. 72 feet 8 inches
     C. 93 feet 6 inches
     D. 102 feet 8 inches

Perimeter:

The perimeter is the distance of the outside edge of an object. To determine the perimeter for a square or rectangle, multiply the length by two (L × 2) and the width by two (W × 2) and then add these two products together: P = (L × 2) + (W × 2)

The correct answer is C.
Each panel is 8 feet 6 inches long, and he needs 11 panels to cover the entire side of the field. So, we need to multiply 8 feet 6 inches by 11, and then simplify the result.
Step 1: 8 feet × 11 = 88 feet
Step 2: 6 inches × 11 = 66 inches
There are 12 inches in a foot, so we need to determine how many feet and inches there are in 66 inches.
66 inches ÷ 12 = 5 feet 6 inches
Step 3: Now add the two results together.
88 feet + 5 feet 6 inches = 93 feet 6 inches

16. A company purchases cell phones at a cost of x and sells the cell phones at four times the cost. Which of the following represents the profit made on each cell phone?
     A. x
     B. $3x$
     C. $4x$
     D. $3 - x$

Profit Calculations:

These types of questions are practical problems that involve buying or selling merchandise. Remember that profit is the difference between the sales price of each unit and the cost of each unit.

The correct answer is B.
The sales price of each cell phone is four times the cost.
The cost is expressed as x, so the sales price is $4x$.
The difference between the sales price of each cell phone and the cost of each cell phone is the profit.
REMEMBER: Sales Price − Cost = Profit

In this problem, the sales price is $4x$ and the cost is x.
$4x - x = $ Profit
$3x = $ Profit

17.   An internet provider sells internet packages based on monthly rates.
The price for the internet service depends on the speed of the internet connection.
The chart that follows indicates the prices of the various internet packages.

Price in dollars (P)	10	20	30	40
Gigabyte speed (s)	2	4	6	8

Which equation represents the prices of these internet packages?
A. $P = (s - 5) \times 5$
B. $P = (s + 5) \times 5$
C. $P = 5 \div s$
D. $P = s \times 5$

The correct answer is D.
The price of the internet connection is always 5 times the speed.
$10 = 2 \times 5$
$20 = 4 \times 5$
$30 = 6 \times 5$
$40 = 8 \times 5$
So, the price of the internet connection (represented by variable P) equals the speed (represented by variable s) times 5.
$P = s \times 5$

18.   Mark owns a bargain bookstore that sells every book for $5. Last week, his sales were $525. This week his sales figure was $600. How many more books did Mark sell this week, compared to last week?
A.   5
B.   15
C.   25
D.   75

Price per Unit:
To calculate price per unit, divide the total cost of the items by the number of units that were purchased.
Price per unit = Total cost ÷ number of units
Conversely: Total cost ÷ price per unit = number of units

The correct answer is B.
The problem tells us that sales this week were $600 and sales last week were $525.
STEP 1: First, we need to find the difference in sales between the two weeks.
$600 − $525 = $75 more in sales this week
STEP 2: Since each book is sold for $5, we divide this figure into the total in order to find out how many books were sold. $75 more sales ÷ $5 per book = 15 more books sold this week

19. Consider a class which has *n* students. In this class, *t*% of the students subscribe to digital TV packages. Which of the following equations represents the number of students who do not subscribe to any digital TV package?

   A. $100(n - t)$

   B. $(100\% - t\%) \times n$

   C. $(100\% - t\%) \div n$

   D. $(1 - t)n$

Percentages and Decimals:

Percentages can be expressed by using the symbol %. They can also be expressed as fractions or decimals.

In general, there are three ways to express percentages.

TYPE 1: Percentages as fractions – Percentages can always be expressed as the number over one hundred.

$$45\% = \frac{45}{100}$$

TYPE 2: Percentages as simplified fractions – Percentages can also be expressed as simplified fractions. In order to simplify the fraction, you have to find the largest number that will go into both the numerator and denominator. In the case of 45%, the fraction is $\frac{45}{100}$, and the numerator and denominator are both divisible by 5. This results in the simplified fraction of $\frac{9}{20}$.

$$\frac{45}{100} = \frac{45 \div 5}{100 \div 5} = \frac{9}{20}$$

TYPE 3: Percentages as decimals – Percentages can also be expressed as decimals.

$$45\% = \frac{45}{100} = 45 \div 100 = 0.45$$

The correct answer is B.

If *t*% subscribe to digital TV packages, then 100% − *t*% do not subscribe. In other words, since a percentage is any given number out of 100%, the percentage of students who do not subscribe is represented by this equation: (100% − *t*%)

This equation is then multiplied by the total number of students (*n*) in order to determine the number of students who do not subscribe to digital TV packages.

$(100\% - t\%) \times n$

20. Find the value of *x* that solves the following proportion: $\frac{3}{6} = \frac{x}{14}$

   A. 3

   B. 6

   C. 7

   D. 9

Proportions:

A proportion is an equation with a ratio on each side. In other words, a proportion is a statement that two ratios are equal. Proportions often involve simplifying fractions, which we have learned how to do in a previous section.

$\frac{3}{4} = \frac{6}{8}$ is an example of a proportion.

We will look at ratios in more depth in the subsequent section.

The correct answer is C.

For proportion problems, you can divide the first fraction by the second fraction. In other words, you can "invert and multiply" or "cross-multiply" to solve.

$$\frac{3}{6} = \frac{x}{14}$$

$$\frac{3}{6} \div \frac{x}{14} =$$

$$\frac{3}{6} \times \frac{14}{x} =$$

$$\frac{3 \times 14}{6x} =$$

$$\frac{42}{6x}$$

The numerator and denominator must be equal when solving proportion problems like this one, so divide to solve: $42 \div 6 = 7$

You can check your answer as follows:
$^3/_6 = {}^7/_{14}$
$^3/_6 \div {}^3/_3 = {}^1/_2$
$^7/_{14} \div {}^7/_7 = {}^1/_2$

21. In a shipment of 100 mp3 players, 1% are faulty.
    What is the ratio of non-faulty mp3 players to faulty mp3 players?
    A. 1:100
    B. 99:100
    C. 1:99
    D. 99:1

Ratios:

Ratios take a group of people or things and divide them into two parts.

For example, if your teacher tells you that each day you should spend two hours studying math for every hour that you spend studying English, you get the ratio 2:1.

Ratios can be expressed as fractions. Ratios can also be expressed by using the colon. For example, a ratio of 2 to 100 can be expressed as $^2/_{100}$ or 2:100.

The number before the colon expresses one subset of the total amount of items.

The number after the colon expresses a different subset of the total.

In other words, when the number before the colon and the number after the colon are added together, we have the total amount of items.

The correct answer is D.
This problem is asking for the quantity of non-faulty mp3 players to the quantity of faulty mp3 players.
Therefore, you must put the quantity of non-faulty mp3 players before the colon in the ratio.
In this problem, 1% of the players are faulty.
1% × 100 = 1 faulty player in every 100 players
100 − 1 = 99 non-faulty players

As explained above, the number before the colon and the number after the colon can be added together to get the total quantity. So, the ratio is 99:1.

22. Jonathan can run 3 miles in 25 minutes. If he maintains this pace, how long will it take him to run 12 miles?
    A. 1 hour and 15 minutes
    B. 1 hour and 40 minutes
    C. 1 hour and 45 minutes
    D. 3 hours

Rate:
Problems on rate may ask you for distance traveled or time spent traveling. You may also see rate questions on production speed, which ask how many units can be produced within a certain time period.

The correct answer is B.

STEP 1: Look to see what information is common to both the question and to the information provided. Here we have the information that he can run 3 miles in 25 minutes. The question is asking how long it will take him to run 12 miles, so the commonality is miles.

STEP 2: Next, you need to find out how many 3-mile increments there are in 12 miles.
$12 \div 3 = 4$

STEP 3: Then you need to determine the time required to travel the stated distance. Accordingly, we need to multiply the time it takes to travel three miles by 4.
25 minutes × 4 = 100
So, 100 minutes are needed to run 12 miles.

STEP 4: Finally, simplify into hours and minutes based on the fact that there are 60 minutes in one hour.
100 minutes = 1 hour 40 minutes

23. The speed of sound in a recent experiment was 340,000 millimeters per second. How far did the sound travel in 1,000 seconds?
    A. 3.4×10^4 millimeters
    B. 3.4×10^5 millimeters
    C. 3.4×10^5 millimeters
    D. 3.4×10^8 millimeters

Scientific Notation:
Scientific notation means that you give the expression as the result of two products: one of which contains a decimal number from 1 to 10, and the other of which contains 10 to an exponential power. The exponent of the 10 is the number of places that the decimal point must be shifted in order to give the number in long form.

The correct answer is D.
Be careful with your zeroes. We are taking 340,000 (4 zeroes) times 1,000 (three zeroes).

The result is: 340,000 × 1,000 = 340,000,000 = 34 × 10,000,000 (seven zeroes). However, our answer choices are expressed with 3.4, not 34.

So, we will need to have to multiply by a figure with 8 zeroes to account for the change in the position of the decimal.

3.4×10^8 millimeters = 3.4 × 100,000,000 millimeters = 340,000,000

24. What is the next number in the following sequence: 1, 5, 9, 13, 17, . . .
    A. 20
    B. 21
    C. 30
    D. 40

Sequences:

Sequences are numbers in a list like the following: 1, 3, 5, 7, 9

In an arithmetic sequence, the difference between one number and the next is known as a constant.

In other words, you add the same value each time until you reach the end of the sequence.

The formula for the nth number of an arithmetic sequence is:

$$a + [d \times (n - 1)]$$

Variable a represents the starting number and variable d represents the difference or constant.

The correct answer is B.

There is a difference of 4 between each number in the above sequence.

Where variable a represents your starting number and variable d represents the difference, you could write an arithmetic sequence like this:

a, a + d, a + 2d, a + 3d, a + 4d, a + 5d, . . .

However, it is easier to remember that the formula for the nth number of an arithmetic sequence is:

a + [d × (n − 1)]

We can prove that 21 is the sixth number of the sequence in our problem by putting the values into the formula.

a = 1

d = 4

n = 6

a + [d × (n − 1)]

1 + [4 × (6 − 1)] =

1 + (4 × 5) =

1 + 20 = 21

You may see sequences involving prime numbers, so you will need to know prime numbers for your exam.

Prime Numbers:

The prime numbers from 1 to 100 are as follows:

2, 3, 5, 7, 11, 13, 17, 19, 23, 29, 31, 37, 41, 43, 47, 53, 59,
61, 67, 71, 73, 79, 83, 89, 97

A prime number is divisible by only two positive integers, itself and 1.

1 is not a prime number because 1 is divisible by only one positive integer, 1.

Square Roots:

A square root is a number that produces a specified result when multiplied by itself. For example, $\sqrt{4} = 2$, because $2 \times 2 = 4$

Be sure to know the following square roots for your exam:

$\sqrt{4} = 2$

$\sqrt{9} = 3$

$\sqrt{16} = 4$

$\sqrt{25} = 5$

$\sqrt{36} = 6$

$\sqrt{49} = 7$

$\sqrt{64} = 8$

$\sqrt{81} = 9$

$\sqrt{100} = 10$

$\sqrt{121} = 11$

$\sqrt{144} = 12$

25. The owner of a carnival attraction launches toy boats of different colors at random. There are 15 boats in total: 5 are blue, 3 are red, and 7 are green. What is the probability that the first boat is blue?

A. $^5/_{14}$

B. $^6/_{14}$

C. $^5/_{15}$

D. $^4/_{15}$

Statistics – Basic Probability:

For basic probability, you need to determine how many chances you have of obtaining the desired outcome (called the event) and divide this number by the number of total possible outcomes (called the sample space).

The correct answer is C.

For questions on probability like this one, you need to determine the quantity of the total sample space.

STEP 1: Determine the total amount in the sample space.

There are 15 boats in total.

5 + 3 + 7 = 15

STEP 2: Determine the amount for the event.

There are 5 blue boats, and a blue boat has not been launched so far, so the event is 5.

STEP 3: The probability is expressed as a fraction.

The amount for the event (5 blue boats) goes on the top of the fraction and the amount of items in the sample space (15 boats in total) goes on the bottom.

So, the answer is $^5/_{15}$. We could also express this in simplified form as $^1/_3$.

Statistics – Arithmetic Mean (Basic Averages):

A basic average, also called the arithmetic mean, is calculated by taking the total of a data set for a group and then dividing this total by the number of people in the group.

For example, have a look at the following problem.
Three people are trying to lose weight. The first person has lost 7 pounds, the second person has lost 10 pounds, and the third person has lost 13 pounds. What is the average weight loss for this group?

STEP 1: Add all of the individual amounts together to get a total for the group.
7 + 10 + 13 = 30

STEP 2: Divide the total from step 1 by the number of people in the group.
30 ÷ 3 = 10
So, the average weight loss is 10 pounds.

However, problems with averages on the ASVAB will quite often be more difficult than the one provided above.
Problems that you see on the exam might involve an average that was calculated in error. Find the total of the data set by reversing the erroneous operation. Then divide the total by the correct number of items in order to find the correct average.
Other types of problems will give you averages for two distinct members of a group, like male and female students in a class, and then ask you to calculate the average for the entire group.

26.   120 students took a math test. The 60 female students in the class had an average score of 95, while the 60 male students in the class had an average of 90. What is the mean score for all 120 students in the class?
A. 75
B. 92.5
C. 93
D. 93.5

Statistics – Advanced Problems on Mean:

For advanced problems on mean, multiply each average by the number of people in each group. Then add the totals for each group together and divide by the total number of people.

The correct answer is B.
STEP 1: You need to find the total points for all the females by multiplying their average by the number of female students.
Then do the same to find the total points for all the males.
Females: 60 × 95 = 5700
Males: 60 × 90 = 5400
STEP 2: Then add these two amounts together to get the total for the group.
5700 + 5400 = 11,100
STEP 3: Then divide by the total number of students in the class to get the overall mean.
11,100 ÷ 120 = 92.5

27. Mark's record of times for the 400 meter freestyle at swim meets this season is:
8.19, 7.59, 8.25, 7.35, 9.10   What is the median of his times?
A. 7.59
B. 8.19
C. 8.25
D. 8.096

Statistics – Median:

Questions may ask you to find the median of a set of numbers. The median is the number that is in the middle of the set when the numbers are in ascending order.

The correct answer is B.
The problem provides the number set: 8.19, 7.59, 8.25, 7.35, 9.10
First of all, put the numbers in ascending order: 7.35, 7.59, 8.19, 8.25, 9.10
Then find the one that is in the middle: 7.35, 7.59, **8.19**, 8.25, 9.10

28. Members of a weight loss group report their individual weight loss to the group leader every week. During the week, these amounts in pounds were reported: 1, 1, 3, 2, 4, 3, 1, 2, and 1. What is the mode of the weight loss for the group?
A. 1 pound
B. 2 pounds
C. 3 pounds
D. 4 pounds

Statistics – Mode:

Mode is the value that occurs most frequently in a data set. For example, if 10 students scored 85 on a test, 6 students scored 90, and 4 students scored 80, the mode score is 85.

The correct answer is A.
The mode is the number that occurs the most frequently in the set.
Our data set is: 1, 1, 3, 2, 4, 3, 1, 2, 1
The number 1 occurs 4 times in the set, which is more frequent than any other number in the set, so the mode is 1.

29. The county is proposing a 7.5% increase in its annual real estate tax. If the tax is currently $480 per year, how much would the tax be if the proposed increase is approved?
A. $444
B. $487
C. $516
D. $840

The correct answer is C.
STEP 1: Calculate the amount of the tax increase.
$480 × 7.5% = ?
$480 original tax amount × 0.075 = $36 proposed increase in tax
STEP 2: Then add the increase to the original amount to get the amount of the tax after the proposed increase.
$480 original tax + $36 increase in tax = $516 tax after increase

30. Sarah wants to create the following conversion: 6 yards = _____ inches
Which of the following is the correct conversion?
A. 6 yards = 18 inches
B. 6 yards = 72 inches
C. 6 yards = 216 inches
D. 6 yards = 864 inches

The correct answer is C.
6 yards × 3 feet per yard = 18 feet
18 feet × 12 inches per foot = 216 inches

ASVAB ARITHMETIC REASONING - PRACTICE TEST 2

In order to simulate exam conditions, you should allow thirty-six minutes to take each practice test.

1. Two people are going to give money to a foundation for a project. Person A will provide one-half of the money. Person B will donate one-eighth of the money. What fraction represents the unfunded portion of the project?
    A. $^1/_{16}$
    B. $^1/_8$
    C. $^1/_4$
    D. $^3/_8$

2. What is the lowest common denominator for the following equation?
    $$\left(\frac{1}{3} + \frac{11}{5}\right) + \left(\frac{1}{15} - \frac{4}{5}\right)$$
    A. 3
    B. 5
    C. 15
    D. 45

3. A hockey team had 50 games this season and lost 20 percent of them. How many games did the team win?
    A. 8
    B. 10
    C. 20
    D. 40

4. Carmen wanted to find the average of the five tests she has taken this semester. She erroneously divided the total points from the five tests by 4, which gave her a result of 90. What is the correct average of her five tests?
    A. 64
    B. 72
    C. 80
    D. 90

5. A census shows that 1,008,942 people live in New Town, and 709,002 people live in Old Town. Which of the following numbers is the best estimate of how many more people live in New Town than in Old Town?
    A. 330,000
    B. 300,000
    C. 33,000
    D. 30,000

6. In a high school, 17 out of every 20 students participate in a sport. If there are 800 students at the high school, what is the total number of students that participate in a sport?
    A. 120 students
    B. 640 students
    C. 680 students
    D. 776 students

7. A new skyscraper is being erected in the city center. The foundation of the building extends 1,135 feet below ground. The building itself, when erected, will measure 13,975 feet above ground. Which of the following is the best estimate of the distance between the deepest point of the foundation below ground and the top of the erected building above ground?
   A. 12,000 feet
   B. 13,000 feet
   C. 14,000 feet
   D. 15,000 feet

8. Mrs. Johnson is going to give candy to the students in her class. The first bag of candy that she has contains 43 pieces. The second contains 28 pieces, and the third contains 31 pieces. If there are 34 students in Mrs. Johnson's class, and the candy is divided equally among all of the students, how many pieces of candy will each student receive?
   A. 3 pieces
   B. 4 pieces
   C. 5 pieces
   D. 51 pieces

9. A town has recently suffered a flood. The total cost, represented by variable C, which is available to accommodate R number of residents in emergency housing is represented by the equation C = $750R + $2,550. If the town has a total of $55,000 available for emergency housing, what is the greatest number of residents that it can house?
   A. 68
   B. 69
   C. 70
   D. 71

10. Two people are going to work on a job. The first person will be paid $7.25 per hour. The second person will be paid $10.50 per hour. A represents the number of hours the first person will work, and B represents the number of hours the second person will work.
    What equation represents the total cost of the wages for this job?
    A. 17.75AB
    B. 17.75 ÷ AB
    C. AB ÷ 17.75
    D. (7.25A + 10.50B)

11. The Johnsons have decided to remodel their upstairs. They currently have 4 rooms upstairs that measure 10 feet by 10 feet each. When they remodel, they will make one large room that will be 20 feet by 10 feet and two small rooms that will each be 10 feet by 8 feet. The remaining space is to be allocated to a new bathroom. What are the dimensions of the new bathroom?
    A. 4 feet × 10 feet
    B. 8 feet × 10 feet
    C. 10 feet × 10 feet
    D. 4 feet × 8 feet

12. Use the table below to answer the following question:

Sunday	Monday	Tuesday	Wednesday	Thursday	Friday	Saturday
−10°F	−9°F	1°F	6°F	8°F	13°F	12°F

The weather forecast for the coming week is given in the table above. What is the difference between the highest and lowest forecasted temperatures for the week?

A. −2°F
B. −3°F
C. 3°F
D. 23°F

13. Acme Packaging uses string to secure their packages prior to shipment. The string is tied around the entire length and entire width of the package, as shown in the following illustration:

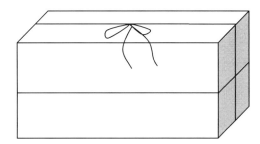

The box is ten inches in height, ten inches in depth, and twenty inches in length. An additional fifteen inches of string is needed to tie a bow on the top of the package. How much string is needed in total in order to tie up the entire package, including making the bow on the top?

A.   55 inches
B.   95 inches
C. 120 inches
D. 135 inches

14. Yesterday a train traveled $117^3/_4$ miles. Today it traveled $102^1/_6$ miles. What is the difference between the distance traveled today and yesterday?

A. 15 miles
B. $15^1/_4$ miles
C. $15^7/_{12}$ miles
D. $15^9/_{12}$ miles

15. During each flight, a flight attendant must count the number of passengers on board the aircraft. The morning flight had 52 passengers more than the evening flight, and there were 540 passengers in total on the two flights that day. How many passengers were there on the evening flight?

A. 244
B. 296
C. 488
D. 540

16. In a math class, $^1/_3$ of the students fail a test. If twelve students have failed the test, how many students are in the class in total?
    A. 15
    B. 16
    C. 36
    D. 38

17. The price of socks is $2 per pair and the price of shoes is $25 per pair. Anna went shopping for socks and shoes, and she paid $85 in total. In this purchase, she bought 3 pairs of shoes. How many pairs of socks did she buy?
    A. 2
    B. 3
    C. 5
    D. 8

18. Terry runs 9 miles every day. If his daily run is rounded up to the nearest 5 miles, which of the following is the best estimate of how many miles he runs every 5 days?
    A. 25
    B. 35
    C. 45
    D. 50

19. Kathy is on a diet. During week 1, she lost 1.07 pounds. During week 2, she lost 2.46 pounds. During week 3, she lost 3.92 pounds. If each week's weight loss amount is rounded up or down to the nearest one-tenth of a pound, what is the estimate of Kathy's weight loss for the entire 3 weeks?
    A. 7 pounds
    B. 7.40 pounds
    C. 7.45 pounds
    D. 7.50 pounds

20. Sandra needs to calculate 16% of 825. Which of the following formulas can she use?
    A. 825×16
    B. 16×825
    C. 825×16
    D. 825×0.16

21. Wayne bought a shirt on sale. The original price of the shirt was $18, and he got a 40% discount. What was the sales price of the shirt?
    A. $7.20
    B. $10.80
    C. $11.80
    D. $17.28

22. Professor Smith uses a system of extra-credit points for his class. Extra-credit points can be offset against the points lost on an exam due to incorrect responses. David answered 18 questions incorrectly on the exam and lost 36 points. He then earned 25 extra credit points. By how much was his exam score ultimately lowered?
    A. –11
    B. 11
    C. 18
    D. 25

23. Which one of the values will correctly satisfy the following mathematical statement: $\frac{2}{3} < ? < \frac{7}{9}$
    A. $\frac{7}{10}$
    B. $\frac{1}{5}$
    C. $\frac{2}{6}$
    D. $\frac{1}{2}$

24. Carl is going to buy a house on an interest-free loan. The total purchase price of the house is represented by variable H. He will pay D dollars immediately, and then he will make equal payments (P) each month for M months. If   H = \$300,000, P = \$700 and M = 360, how much will Carl pay immediately?
    A.   \$38,000
    B.   \$48,000
    C.   \$58,000
    D.   \$252,000

25. $8^7 \times 8^3 = ?$
    A. 8^4
    B. 8^{10}
    C. 8^{21}
    D. 64^{10}

26. Express the following number in scientific notation: 625
    A. $\log 625$
    B. $\log 625 \times 10^2$
    C. 62.5×10
    D. 6.25×10^2

27. What number is next in the sequence 7, 14, 21, 28
    A. 35
    B. 42
    C. 49
    D. 56

28. What is the result of the following: 4!
    A. 12
    B. 16
    C. 24
    D. 36

29. A die is rolled and a coin is tossed. What is the probability that the die shows an even number and the coin shows tails?

A. $1/2$

B. $1/4$

C. $1/6$

D. $1/12$

30. Return on investment (ROI) percentages are provided for seven companies. The ROI will be negative if the company operated at a loss, but the ROI will be a positive value if the company operated at a profit. The ROI's for the seven companies were:

−2%, 5%, 7.5%, 14%, 17%, 1.3%, −3%.

Which figure below best approximates the mean ROI for the seven companies?

A. 2%

B. 5.7%

C. 6.25%

D. 7.5%

Practice Test 2 – Answers

1. D
2. C
3. D
4. B
5. B
6. C
7. D
8. A
9. B
10. D
11. A
12. D
13. D
14. C
15. A
16. C
17. C
18. D
19. D
20. D
21. B
22. B
23. A
24. B
25. B
26. D
27. A
28. C
29. B
30. B

Practice Test 2 – Explanations for the Answers

1. The correct answer is D.

You will see practical problems involving fractions like this one on the exam.

The sum of all contributions must be equal to 100%, simplified to 1.

STEP 1: Set up an equation. Let's say that the variable U represents the unfunded portion of the project.

So, the equation that represents this problem is. $A + B + U = 1$

STEP 2: Substitute with the fractions that have been provided.

$$\frac{1}{2} + \frac{1}{8} + U = 1$$

STEP 3: Find the lowest common denominator (LCD). Finding the lowest common denominator means that you have to make all of the numbers on the bottoms of the fractions the same. Remember that you need to find the common factors of the denominators in order to find the LCD.

We know that 2 and 4 are factors of 8 because 2 × 4 = 8.

So, the LCD for this question is 8 since the denominator of the first fraction is 2 and because 2 is a factor of 8.

STEP 4: Convert the fractions into the lowest common denominator to solve the problem. We put the fractions into the LCD as follows:

$$\frac{1}{2} + \frac{1}{8} + U = 1$$

$$\left(\frac{1}{2} \times \frac{4}{4}\right) + \frac{1}{8} + U = 1$$

$$\frac{4}{8} + \frac{1}{8} + U = 1$$

$$\frac{5}{8} + U = 1$$

$$\frac{5}{8} - \frac{5}{8} + U = 1 - \frac{5}{8}$$

$$U = 1 - \frac{5}{8}$$

$$U = \frac{8}{8} - \frac{5}{8}$$

$$U = \frac{3}{8}$$

2. The correct answer is C.

We have to find the lowest common denominator (LCD) of the fractions. The LCD for this question is 15. We know this because the product of the other denominators is 3 times 5, which is 15.

We can illustrate the solution as follows:

$$\left(\frac{1}{3}+\frac{11}{5}\right)+\left(\frac{1}{15}-\frac{4}{5}\right)=$$

$$\left[\left(\frac{1}{3}\times\frac{5}{5}\right)+\left(\frac{11}{5}\times\frac{3}{3}\right)\right]+\left[\frac{1}{15}-\left(\frac{4}{5}\times\frac{3}{3}\right)\right]=$$

$$\frac{5}{15}+\frac{33}{15}+\frac{1}{15}-\frac{12}{15}$$

3. The correct answer is D.

For practical problems like this, you must first determine the percentage and formula that you need in order to solve the problem.

Then, you must do multiplication to determine how many games the team won.

However, the question tells you the percentage of games the team lost, not won.

STEP 1: First of all, we have to calculate the percentage of games won.

If the team lost 20 percent of the games, we know that the team won the remaining 80 percent.

STEP 2: Now do the multiplication.

  50 games in total

× .80 percentage of games won (in decimal form)

 40.0 total games won

4. The correct answer is B.

STEP 1: First you need to find the total points that the student earned. You do this by taking Carmen's erroneous average times 4.

4 × 90 = 360

STEP 2: Then you need to divide the total points earned by the correct number of tests in order to get the correct average.

360 ÷ 5 = 72

5. The correct answer is B.

This is one type of estimation question.

The problem tells us that 1,008,942 people live in New Town, and 709,002 people live in Old Town.

STEP 1: We need to round the numbers up or down to the nearest thousand, since the answer choices are expressed to the nearest thousand.

1,008,942 is rounded to 1,009,000

709,002 is rounded to 709,000

STEP 2: Then subtract the second figure from the first figure in order to get your result.

1,009,000 − 709,000 = 300,000

6. The correct answer is C.

Remember that for questions like this one, you have to find the commonality between the facts in the question and the requested information for the solution.

In this question, the commonality is the number of students.

The question tells us that 17 out of every 20 students participate in a sport and that there are 800 total students.

STEP 1: Determine how many groups of 20 can be formed from the total of 800.

800 ÷ 20 = 40 groups of 20 students in the school

STEP 2: To solve the problem, you then need to multiply the number of participants per group by the possible number of groups.

In this problem, there are 17 participants per every group of 20.

There are 40 groups of 20.

So, we multiply 17 by 40 to get our answer.

17 × 40 = 680 students

7. The correct answer is D.

The foundation of the building extends 1,135 feet below ground. The building itself, when erected, will measure 13,975 feet above ground.

STEP 1: Look at the answer options in order to determine what rounding is required.

Here, we see that the answer options are in increments of one thousand.

STEP 2: Perform the rounding on both figures.

So, we round each number up or down to the nearest thousand.

1,135 is rounded down to 1,000

13,975 is rounded up to 14,000

STEP 3: Perform the necessary mathematical computation.

We add the two figures together from above in order to get our result.

1,000 + 14,000 = 15,000

8. The correct answer is A.

STEP 1: First of all, we need to find out how many pieces of candy there are in total.

43 + 28 + 31 = 102 total pieces of candy

STEP 2: We need to divide the total amount of candy by the number of students in order to find out how much candy each student will get.

102 total pieces of candy ÷ 34 students = 3 pieces of candy per student

9. The correct answer is B.

The total amount available is $55,000, so we can substitute this for C in the equation provided in order to calculate R number of residents:

$C = \$750R + \$2,550$

$\$55,000 = \$750R + \$2,550$

$\$55,000 - \$2,550 = \$750R + \$2,550 - \$2,550$

$\$55,000 - \$2,550 = \$750R$

$\$52,450 = \$750R$

$\$52,450 ÷ \$750 = \$750R ÷ \$750$

$\$52,450 ÷ \$750 = R$

$69.9 = R$

It is not possible to accommodate a fractional part of one person, so we need to round down to 69 residents.

10. The correct answer is D.

STEP 1: Assign variables as necessary. The two people are working at different costs per hour, so each person needs to be assigned a variable. A is for the number of hours for the first person, and B is for the number of hours for the second person.

STEP 2: The cost for each person is calculated by taking the number of hours that the person works by the hourly wage for that person.

So, the equation for wages for the first person is (7.25 × A)

The equation for the wages for the second person is (10.50 × B)

STEP 3: The total cost of the wages for this job is the sum of the wages of these two people.

(7.25 × A) + (10.50 × B) =

(7.25A + 10.50B)

11. The correct answer is A.

STEP 1: First, we have to calculate the total square footage available. If there are 4 rooms which are 10 by 10 each, we have this equation:

$4 \times (10 \times 10) = 400$ square feet in total

STEP 2: Now calculate the square footage of the new rooms.

$20 \times 10 = 200$

2 rooms $\times (10 \times 8) = 160$

$200 + 160 = 360$ total square feet for the new rooms

STEP 3: The remaining square footage for the bathroom is calculated by taking the total minus the square footage of the new rooms.

$400 - 360 = 40$ square feet

Since each existing room is 10 feet long, we know that the new bathroom also needs to be 10 feet long in order to fit in. So, the new bathroom is 4 feet × 10 feet.

12. The correct answer is D.

The lowest temperature is −10°F, and the highest temperature is 13°F.

The difference between these two figures is calculated by subtracting.

Be careful when you subtract. In particular, remember that when you see two negative signs together, you need to add because two negatives make a positive.

$13 - (-10) =$

$13 + 10 = 23$

13. The correct answer is D.

For questions that ask you about tying string around a package, you will need to consider the length, height, and depth of the package when doing your calculation.

STEP 1: The string that goes around the top, bottom, and ends of the package will be measured as follows: 20 + 10 + 20 + 10 = 60 inches

STEP 2: The string that goes around the front and back sides and the ends of the package will be calculated similarly since the front and back sides are of the course the same length as the top and bottom.

20 + 10 + 20 + 10 = 60 inches

STEP 3: Don't forget that an additional fifteen inches of rope is needed to tie a bow on the top of the package.

STEP 4: We add these three amounts together to get our total.

60 + 60 + 15 = 135 inches

14. The correct answer is C.

Yesterday the train traveled $117^3/_4$ miles, and today it traveled $102^1/_6$ miles. To find the difference, we subtract these two amounts. Because the fraction on the first mixed number is greater than the fraction on the second mixed number, we can subtract the whole numbers and the fractions separately.

$117^3/_4$ miles – $102^1/_6$ miles = ?

STEP 1: Subtract the whole numbers.

117 – 102 = 15 miles

STEP 2: Perform the operation on the fractions by finding the lowest common denominator.

$^3/_4$ miles – $^1/_6$ miles = ?

In order to find the LCD, we need to find the common factors first.

Our denominators in this problem are 4 and 6.

The factors of 4 are:

1 × 4 = 4

2 × 2 = 4

The factors of 6 are:

1 × 6 = 6

2 × 3 = 6

We do not have two factors in common, so we know that we need to find a new denominator which is greater than 6.

In this problem, the LCD is 12 since 3 × 4 = 12 and 2 × 6 = 12.

So, we express the fractions $^3/_4$ miles + $^1/_6$ miles from above in their LCD form.

$^3/_4 \times ^3/_3 = ^9/_{12}$

$^1/_6 \times ^2/_2 = ^2/_{12}$

Then subtract these two fractions.

$^9/_{12} – ^2/_{12} = ^7/_{12}$

STEP 3: Combine the results from the two previous steps to solve the problem.

$117^3/_4$ miles – $102^1/_6$ miles =

$117^9/_{12}$ miles – $102^2/_{12}$ miles =

$15^7/_{12}$ miles

15. The correct answer is A.

The problem tells us that the morning flight had 52 passengers more than the evening flight, and there were 540 passengers in total on the two flights that day.

STEP 1: First of all, we need to deduct the difference from the total:

540 – 52 = 488

In other words, there were 488 passengers on both flights combined, plus the 52 additional passengers on the morning flight.

STEP 2: Now divide this result by 2 to allocate the amount of passengers to each flight.

488 ÷ 2 = 244 passengers on the evening flight

So, the evening flight had 244 passengers

Had the question asked you for the amount of passengers on the morning flight, you would have had to add back the amount of additional passengers to find the total amount of passengers for the morning flight.

244 + 52 = 296 passengers on the morning flight

16. The correct answer is C.

The twelve students who failed the test represent one-third of the class. Since one-third of the students have failed, we can think of the class as being divided into three groups:

Group 1: The 12 students who failed

Group 2: 12 students who would have passed

Group 3: 12 more students who would have passed

So, the class consists of 36 students in total.

In other words, we need to multiply by three to find the total number of students.

12 × 3 = 36

Alternatively, we can divide by the fraction to solve:

$12 \div \frac{1}{3} =$

$12 \times \frac{3}{1} =$

12 × 3 =

36

17. The correct answer is C.

Assign a different variable to each item, and then make an equation by multiplying each variable by its price.

STEP 1: Assign the variables.

Let's say that the number of pairs of socks is S and the number of pairs of shoes is H.

STEP 2: Set up your equation.

Your equation is: $(S \times \$2) + (H \times \$25) = \$85$

STEP 3: We know that the number of pairs of shoes is 3, so put that in the equation and solve it.

$(S \times \$2) + (H \times \$25) = \$85$

$(S \times \$2) + (3 \times \$25) = \$85$

$(S \times \$2) + \$75 = \$85$

$(S \times \$2) + 75 - 75 = \$85 - \$75$

$(S \times \$2) = \$10$

$\$2S = \$10$

$\$2S \div 2 = \$10 \div 2$

$S = 5$

18. The correct answer is D.

STEP 1: Looking at the answer choices, we can see that we need to round to the nearest increment of 5.

So, for this problem, think about the increments of 5:

5, 10, 15, 20, 25, etc.

STEP 2. Perform the rounding.

9 miles per day is rounded up to 10 miles per day.

STEP 3: Multiply to find the solution.

We then multiply this figure by the number of days to get our result.

10 miles per day × 5 days = 50 miles every five days

19. The correct answer is D.

One-tenth is expressed is decimal form like this: 0.1

So, any amount that has a decimal less than 0.05 is rounded down and decimals of 0.05 and greater are rounded up.

STEP 1: We do the rounding as follows:

1.07 is rounded up to 1.1

2.46 is rounded up to 2.5

3.92 is rounded down to 3.9

STEP 2: Then add the rounded figures together to get your result.

1.1 + 2.5 + 3.9 = 7.5

20. The correct answer is D.

A percentage can always be expressed as a number with two decimal places.

For example, 15% = 0.15 and 20% = 0.20

In our problem, 16% = 0.16

So, 16% of 825 = 825 × 0.16.

21. The correct answer is B.

STEP 1: First of all, you need to calculate the amount of the discount.

$18 original price × 40% =

$18 × 0.40 = $7.20 discount

STEP 2: Then deduct the amount of the discount from the original price to calculate the sales price of the item.

$18 original price - $7.20 discount = $10.80 sales price

22. The correct answer is B.

If David answered 18 questions incorrectly on the exam and lost 36 points, and he then earned 25 extra credit points, his score was lowered by 11 points.

STEP 1: To do the calculation, we need to take the points lost on the exam and add the extra credit points.

−36 + 25 = −11

STEP 2: Since the question is asking how much the score was lowered, you need to give the amount as a positive number.

23. The correct answer is A.

This question involves common denominators.

The question is: $^2/_3 < ? < ^7/_9$

STEP 1: First of all, we need to find a common denominator for the fractions in the equation, as well as for all of the answer choices. In order to complete the problem quickly, you should not try to find the lowest common denominator, but just find any common denominator.

We can do this by expressing all of the numbers with a denominator of 90 since 9 is the largest denominator in the equation and 10 is the largest denominator in the answer choices.

$\frac{2}{3} \times \frac{30}{30} = \frac{60}{90}$

$\frac{7}{9} \times \frac{10}{10} = \frac{70}{90}$

STEP 2: Then, express the original equation in terms of the common denominator.

$\frac{60}{90} < ? < \frac{70}{90}$

STEP 3: Then express the answer choices in terms of the common denominator.

A. $\frac{7}{10} \times \frac{9}{9} = \frac{63}{90}$

B. $\frac{1}{5} \times \frac{18}{18} = \frac{18}{90}$

C. $\frac{2}{6} \times \frac{15}{15} = \frac{30}{90}$

D. $\frac{1}{2} \times \frac{45}{45} = \frac{45}{90}$

STEP 4: Compare the results to find the answer.

By comparing the numerators (the top numbers of the fractions), we can see that $\frac{63}{90}$ lies between $\frac{60}{90}$ and $\frac{70}{90}$, so A is the correct answer.

24. The correct answer is B.

The total of the monthly payments is:

$700 per month × 360 months = $252,000

The total price of the house is $300,000 so deduct the total payments from this amount in order to calculate the immediate payment: $300,000 − $252,000 = $48,000

25. The correct answer is B.

This question tests your knowledge of exponent laws.

First look to see whether your base number is the same on each part of the equation.

In this question, 8 is the base number for each part of the equation. If the base number is the same, and the problem asks you to multiply, you simply add the exponents.

$8^7 \times 8^3 = 8^{(7+3)} = 8^{10}$

26. The correct answer is D.

Scientific notation means that you have to give the number as the product of a multiple of 10 to an exponential power and a number between 1 and 10.

So, the answer is 6.25×10^2.

27. The correct answer is A.

First, find the relationship between each of the numbers.

7 + 7 = 14

14 + 7 = 21

21 + 7 = 28

Therefore, we have to add 7 to 28 in order to find the solution.

28 + 7 = 35

28. The correct answer is C.

This type of problem is known as a factorial. When you see the exclamation point, you need to multiply the number given by every lesser number, as shown below.

$4! = (4 \times 3 \times 2 \times 1) = 24$

29. The correct answer is B.

The die has six numbers, from 1 to 6, and the coin has two outcomes, heads (H) or tails (T).

Therefore, the sample space can be expressed as follows:

(1,H),(2,H),(3,H),(4,H),(5,H),(6,H), (1,T),(2,T),(3,T),(4,T),(5,T),(6,T)

Counting the items in the above set, we can see that there are 12 items in total.

The desired outcome or "event" is that the die shows an even number and the coin shows a tails.

The possible outcomes are: {(2,T),(4,T),(6,T)}

So, the probability is: $^3/_{12} = {}^1/_4$

30. The correct answer is B.

The mean is the arithmetic average.

First, add up all of the items:

−2% + 5% + 7.5% + 14% + 17% + 1.3% + −3% = 39.8%.

Then divide by 7 since there are 7 companies in the set: 39.8% ÷ 7 = 5.68% ≈ 5.7%

ASVAB ARITHMETIC REASONING - PRACTICE TEST 3

1. Shanika works as a car salesperson. She earns $1,000 a month, plus $390 for each car she sells. If she wants to earn at least $4,000 this month, what is the minimum number of cars that she must sell this month?
   A. 6
   B. 7
   C. 8
   D. 9

2. The university bookstore is having a sale. Course books can be purchased for $40 each, or 5 books can be purchased for a total of $150. How much would a student save on each book if he or she purchased 5 books?
   A. 5
   B. 10
   C. 50
   D. 90

3. A car uses gasoline at the rate of 25 miles per gallon. The car travels for 5 hours at a speed of 55 miles per hour. If gas costs $3 per gallon, how much will the gasoline cost for this trip?
   A. 25
   B. 33
   C. 45
   D. 75

4. Tom bought a shirt on sale for $12. The original price of the shirt was $15. What was the percentage of the discount on the sale?
   A. 2%
   B. 3%
   C. 20%
   D. 25%

5. A car travels at 60 miles per hour. The car is currently 240 miles from Denver. How long will it take for the car to get to Denver?
   A. 40 minutes
   B. 60 minutes
   C. 4 hours
   D. 5 hours

6. Mrs. Ramirez is inviting 12 children to her son's birthday party. The children will play pin the tail on the donkey. Mrs. Ramirez has already made 40 tails for the game. She wants to give each child 4 tails to play the game. How many more tails does she need to make?
   A. 4
   B. 8
   C. 10
   D. 12

7.   Use the diagram below to answer the question that follows.

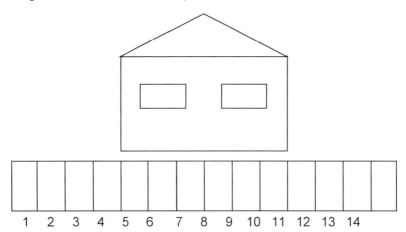

| | 1 | 2 | 3 | 4 | 5 | 6 | 7 | 8 | 9 | 10 | 11 | 12 | 13 | 14 |

If each rectangle in the ruler below the picture of the house is one unit and the actual length of the house is 36 feet, then what is the scale of the diagram of the house?
A.   1 unit = 6 feet
B.   1 unit = 7.2 feet
C.   1 unit = 9 feet
D.   1 unit = 12 feet

8.   Sharon's pancake recipe calls for 2 cups of milk. How many ounces of milk will she need for this recipe?
A.   4 ounces
B.   8 ounces
C.   16 ounces
D.   32 ounces

9.   A class contains 20 students. On Tuesday 5% of the students were absent. On Wednesday 20% of the students were absent. How many more students were absent on Wednesday than on Tuesday?
A.   1
B.   2
C.   3
D.   4

10. Pat wants to put wooden trim around the floor of her family room. Each piece of wood is 1 foot in length. The room is rectangular and is 12 feet long and 10 feet wide. How many pieces of wood does Pat need for the entire perimeter of the room?
A.   22
B.   44
C.   100
D.   120

11. Ben uses one bag of dog food every 6 days to feed his dog. Approximately how many bags of dog food would Ben require for two months?
   A. 5
   B. 6
   C. 9
   D. 10

12. The snowfall for November is 5 inches less than for December. If the total snowfall for November and December is 35 inches, what was the snowfall for November?
   A. 10 inches
   B. 15 inches
   C. 20 inches
   D. 30 inches

13. Records indicate that there were 12 hospitals in Johnson County in 1995, but this number had increased to 15 hospitals in 2015. There were 12 births on average per hospital in Johnson County in 1995. The total number of births in Johnson County was 240 in 2015. By what amount does the average number of births per hospital in Johnson County for 2015 exceed those for 1995?
   A. 3 births per hospital
   B. 4 births per hospital
   C. 15 births per hospital
   D. 16 births per hospital

14. A magician has a bag of colored scarves for a magic trick that he performs. The bag contains 3 blue scarves, 1 red scarf, 4 green scarves, and 2 orange scarves. If the magician removes scarves at random, what is the probability that the first scarf will be orange?
   A. $^1/_2$
   B. $^2/_7$
   C. $^1/_{10}$
   D. $^2/_{10}$

15. Marta can walk one mile in 17 minutes. At this rate, how long would it take her to walk 5 miles?
   A. 1 hour and 25 minutes
   B. 1 hour and 8 minutes
   C. 1 hour and 7 minutes
   D. 1 hour and 5 minutes

16. **Use the information below to answer the question that follows.**

Appleton	Brownsville	Charlestown	Durham	Easton
687 feet below sea level	1586 feet above sea level	253 feet below sea level	542 feet below sea level	1621 feet above sea level

As part of a geography class, students are required to learn the distance above and below sea level of certain towns in their area. What was the difference in feet between the highest and lowest towns in their area according to the above table?

A. 66 feet

B. 621 feet

C. 874 feet

D. 2308 feet

17. Clark County had 135,298 cases of infectious disease last year, while Davidson County had 207,121 cases. What number is the best estimate of how many more cases of infectious disease there were in Davidson County?

A. 12,000

B. 62,000

C. 72,000

D. 74,000

18. If six people can paint a house in two days, how long will it take two people to do the same job?

A. 4 days

B. 4 and a half days

C. 6 days

D. 6 and a half days

19. Sam's final grade for a class is based on his scores from a midterm test (M), a project (P), and a final exam (F). The midterm test counts twice as much as the project, and the final exam counts twice as much as the midterm. Which mathematical expression below can be used to calculate Sam's final grade?

A. P + M + F

B. P + 2M + 4F

C. P + 2M + F

D. P + M + 2F

20. Bart is riding his bike at a rate of 12 miles per hour. He arrives in the town of Wilmington at 3:00 pm. The town of Mount Pleasant is 50 miles from Wilmington. How far will Bart be from Mount Pleasant at 5:00 pm if he continues riding his bike at this speed?

A. 12 miles

B. 20 miles

C. 24 miles

D. 26 miles

21. A ticket office sold 360 more tickets on Friday than it did on Saturday. If the office sold 2570 tickets in total during Friday and Saturday, how many tickets did it sell on Friday?

A. 360

B. 1105

C. 1465

D. 1565

22. Tom's height increased by 10% this year. If Tom was 5 feet tall at the beginning of the year, how tall is he now?
    A. 5 feet 1 inch
    B. 5 feet 5 inches
    C. 5 feet 6 inches
    D. 5 feet 10 inches

23. Carlos buys 2 pairs of jeans for $22.98 each. He later decides to exchange both pairs of jeans for 3 sweaters which cost $15.50 each. Which equation can Carlos use to calculate the extra money he will have to pay for the exchange?
    A. 2 × (22.98 - 15.50)
    B. 3 × (22.98 - 15.50)
    C. (3 × 22.98) – (2 × 15.50)
    D. (3 × 15.50) – (2 × 22.98)

24. A museum counts its visitors each day and rounds each daily figure up or down to the nearest 5 people. 104 people visit the museum on Monday, 86 people visit the museum on Tuesday, and 81 people visit the museum on Wednesday. Which figure below best represents the amount of visitors to the museum for the three days, after rounding?
    A. 260
    B. 265
    C. 270
    D. 275

25. Jason does the high jump for his high school track and field team. His first jump is at 3.246 meters. His second is 3.331 meters, and his third is 3.328 meters. If the height of each jump is rounded to the nearest one-hundredth of a meter (also called a centimeter), what is the estimate of the total height for all three jumps combined?
    A.   9.80 meters
    B.   9.89 meters
    C.   9.90 meters
    D.   9.91 meters

26. Use the table below to answer the question that follows.

Regional Railway Train Service	
Departure Time	Arrival Time
9:50 am	10:36 am
11:15 am	12:01 pm
12:30 pm	1:16 pm
2:15 pm	3:01 pm
?	5:51 pm

The journey on the Regional Railway is always exactly the same duration.
What is the missing time in the chart above?
    A. 3:30 pm
    B. 4:15 pm
    C. 4:30 pm
    D. 5:05 pm

27. What is the median of the numbers in the following list?
    1.6, 2.9, 4.5, 2.5, 2.5, 5.1, 5.4
    A. 2.9
    B. 2.5
    C. 3.5
    D. 3.1

28. An electricity company measures the energy consumption for each home in kilowatt hours (KWH). During July, the homes in one street had the levels of consumption in KWH in the chart show below. What is the mode of the level of energy consumption for this neighborhood for July?

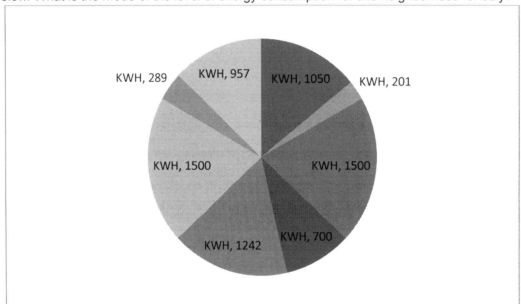

    A. 700 KWH
    B. 957 KWH
    C. 828.5 KWH
    D. 1500 KWH

29. What number is next? 3, 5, 7, 11
    A. 13
    B. 14
    C. 16
    D. 18

30. A jar contains 4 red marbles, 6 green marbles, and 10 white marbles. If a marble is drawn from the jar at random, what is the probability that this marble is white?
    A. $1/2$
    B. $1/5$
    C. $1/10$
    D. $3/10$

Practice Test 3 – Answers

1. C

2. B

3. B

4. C

5. C

6. B

7. A

8. C

9. C

10. B

11. D

12. B

13. B

14. D

15. A

16. D

17. C

18. C

19. B

20. D

21. C

22. C

23. D

24. C

25. D

26. D

27. A

28. D

29. A

30. A

Practice Test 3 – Explanations for the Answers

1. The correct answer is C.

Shanika wants to earn $4,000 this month. She gets the $1,000 basic pay regardless of the number of cars she sells, so we need to subtract that from the total first: $4,000 − $1,000 = $3,000.

She gets $390 for each car she sells, so we need to divide that into the remaining $3,000:

$3,000 to earn ÷ $390 per car = 7.69 cars to sell

Since it is not possible to sell a part of a car, we need to round up to 8 cars.

2. The correct answer is B.

First, divide the total price for the multi-purchase by the number of items.

In this case, $150 ÷ 5 = $30 for each of the five books.

Then, subtract this amount from the original price to get your answer.

$40 − $30 = $10

Alternatively, you can use the method explained below.

Calculate the total price for the five books without the discount.

5 × $40 = $200

Then subtract the discounted price of $150 from the total.

$200 - $150 = $50

Then divide the total savings by the number of books to determine the savings on each book.

$50 total savings ÷ 5 books = $10 savings per book

3. The correct answer is B.

First, you need to find the total miles traveled.

5 hours × 55 miles per hour = 275 miles traveled

Then divide the miles traveled by the miles per gallon in order to find out how many gallons of gas were used during the trip.

275 miles traveled ÷ 25 miles per gallon = 11 gallons

Then multiply by the cost per gallon in order to determine the total cost.

11 gallons used × $3 per gallon = $33 in total

4. The correct answer is C.

Find the dollar amount of the discount first.

$15 original price − $12 sales price = $3 discount

Then divide the discount into the original price to get the percentage.

$3 ÷ $15 = 0.20 = 20%

5. The correct answer is C.

Divide the miles per hour into the distance left in order to get the time needed.

240 miles remaining ÷ 60 mph = 4 hours left to travel

6. The correct answer is B.

If there are 12 children and each one is supposed to receive 4 items, we can do the calculation as follows:

12 children × 4 items per child = 48 items required in total

Now subtract the total from the amount she has already made in order to determine how many more she needs.

48 items required in total – 40 items available = 8 items still needed

7. The correct answer is A.

Count the number of units that the house spans, rather than trying to subtract units from the total of 14.

If we count the number of units below the house in the drawing, we can see that the house spans 6 units.

Divide this result into the actual length of the house (36 feet) to get the scale of the drawing.

36 feet ÷ 6 units = 6 feet represented by each unit

8. The correct answer is C.

The recipe calls for 2 cups of milk. There are 8 ounces in one cup, so we need to multiply in order to find the answer:

2 cups × 8 ounces per cup = 16 ounces in total

9. The correct answer is C.

First of all, you have to find out how many students were absent on Tuesday. To find the number of absent students, you have to multiply the total number of students in the class by the percentage of the absence for Tuesday.

20 students in total × 5% = 1 student absent on Tuesday

Now calculate the absences for Wednesday in the same way.

20 students in total × 20% = 4 students absent on Wednesday

The problem is asking you how many more students were absent on Wednesday than Tuesday, so you need to subtract the two figures that you have just calculated above.

4 students absent on Wednesday – 1 student absent on Tuesday = 3 students

So, 3 more students were absent on Wednesday than Tuesday.

10. The correct answer is B.

Remember that the perimeter is the measurement along the outside edges of the rectangle or other area.

The formula for perimeter is as follows:

P = 2W + 2L

If the room is 12 feet by 10 feet, we need 12 feet × 2 feet to finish the long sides of the room and 10 feet × 2 feet to finish the shorter sides of the room.

(2 × 10) + (2 × 12) =

20 + 24 = 44

11. The correct answer is D.

Most months have 30 or 31 days. In this problem, we are being asked to do a calculation for a 2-month period, so we are dealing with 60 to 62 days.

For the purposes of estimation, we can use 60 days.

Ben uses a bag of dog food every 6 days.

So, we divide the total period by the number of days to get the required amount.

60 day period ÷ 6 days each bag = 10 bags needed for 60 days

12. The correct answer is B.

You will notice in this problem that we are dealing with two months, November and December.

STEP 1: Look at the total.

The total for the two months is 35 inches.

STEP 2: Determine whether one month is higher than the other.

In this problem, one month has 5 inches more than the other, so you have to subtract the difference first of all.

35 − 5 = 30

STEP 3: Now divide this amount by two to allocate each part to the two months.

30 ÷ 2 = 15

STEP 4: Look again at the problem to see if you are calculating the amount for the high month or the low month.

Here, the amount for November is lower than the amount for December.

So, we know that November had 15 inches of snowfall.

If the problem had asked for the higher month, you would then need to add back the difference.

So, December's snowfall is 15 + 5 = 20

STEP 5: Check your result by adding the amounts for the two months together.

15 + 20 = 35

13. The correct answer is B.

The problem is asking you for the amount that the average number of births per hospital in Johnson County for 2015 exceeded those for 1995.

STEP 1: First we have to calculate the average for 2015.

In order to calculate an average, you have to divide the total amount by the number of items in each data set.

For 2015, we have 240 total births and 15 hospitals in the data set.

240 ÷ 15 = 16 births on average per hospital for 2015

STEP 2: Now calculate the average for 1995

In our problem, this average is provided.

We can see that there were 12 births on average per hospital in Johnson County in 1995.

STEP 3: Now subtract the averages for the two years to get your answer.

16 − 12 = 4 more births per hospital in 2015

14. The correct answer is D.

STEP 1: Determine the total amount in the sample space. Here, we have a bag that contains 3 blue scarves, 1 red scarf, 4 green scarves, and 2 orange scarves.

3 + 1 + 4 + 2 = 10 items in the sample space

STEP 2: Determine the amount for the event.

The problem is asking for the chance of getting an orange scarf. So, we have 2 orange scarves for the event.

STEP 3: The probability is expressed as a fraction. The amount in the event (2 orange scarves) goes on the top of the fraction and the amount of items in the sample space (10 items) goes on the bottom.

So, the answer is $^2/_{10}$. This could be simplified and expressed as $^1/_5$.

15. The correct answer is A.

STEP 1: You need to multiply the number of miles that she is going to travel by the amount of time it takes her to travel one mile.

17 minutes for 1 mile × 5 miles to travel = 85 minutes needed

STEP 2: Now express the result in hours and minutes, remembering of course that an hour has 60 minutes.

85 minutes – 60 minutes = 25 minutes

So, the answer is 1 hour and 25 minutes.

16. The correct answer is D.

STEP 1: Look at the chart to see which town is the highest.

Here, Easton is the highest at 1621 feet above sea level.

STEP 2: Look at the chart to see which town is the lowest.

Appleton is the lowest at 687 feet below sea level.

STEP 3: Now subtract these two amounts together to find the total distance between the high point and the low point.

1621 – (–687) =

1621 + 687 = 2308

17. The correct answer is C.

The problem tells us that Clark County had 135,298 cases of infectious disease last year, while Davidson County had 207,121 cases.

STEP 1: Round each number up or down to the nearest thousand.

207,121 is rounded down to 207,000.

135,298 is rounded down to 135,000.

STEP 2: Subtract the two figures to estimate the difference.

207,000 – 135,000 = 72,000

18. The correct answer is C.

Six people can paint a house in two days, but we have only two people.

So we need to divide first of all.

6 people ÷ 2 people = 3 times the days needed to do the job

Then multiply to determine how long it will take two people to do the same job.

2 people × 3 times the days needed to do the job = 6 days

19. The correct answer is B.

Sam's final grade for a class is based on his scores from a midterm test (M), a project (P), and a final exam (F), but the midterm test counts twice as much as the project, and the final exam counts twice as much as the midterm. Therefore, we have to count variable M twice.

The value of the midterm is doubled and variable F is double of the midterm, so we have to count variable F 4 times.

So, the equation is: P + 2M + 4F

20. The correct answer is D.

The problem tells us that Bart rides at a rate of 12 miles per hour. We also know that he arrives in the town of Wilmington at 3:00 pm. The question is asking us how far Bart will be from Mount Pleasant at 5:00 pm.

STEP 1: Calculate the time difference.

5:00 pm – 3:00 pm = 2 hours difference

STEP 2: Calculate the distance traveled.

12 miles per hour × 2 hours = 24 miles traveled

STEP 3: Calculate the distance left.

The town of Mount Pleasant is 50 miles from Wilmington.

50 miles to travel – 24 miles traveled = 26 miles left

21. The correct answer is C.

The ticket office sold 360 more tickets on Friday than it did on Saturday. The office sold 2570 tickets in total during Friday and Saturday.

STEP 1: Subtract the excess.

2570 – 360 = 2210

STEP 2: Allocate the above figure to each day.

2210 ÷ 2 = 1105

STEP 3: Calculate Friday's amount by adding back in the excess.

1105 + 360 = 1465

22. The correct answer is C.

Tom was 5 feet tall at the beginning of the year, and his height increased by 10% this year.

STEP 1: Calculate the beginning height in inches. Remember that there are 12 inches in a foot.

5 feet × 12 inches per foot = 60 inches in height

STEP 2: Calculate the increase in height.

60 inches × 10% = 6 inches

STEP 3: Calculate the new height by adding the increase to the number at the beginning.

5 feet + 6 inches = 5 feet 6 inches

23. The correct answer is D.

The problem tells us that Carlos buys 2 pairs of jeans for $22.98 each, and then he decides to exchange both pairs of jeans for 3 sweaters which cost $15.50 each.

STEP 1: Calculate the amount of money spent on the original purchase of the jeans.

2 × $22.98 = $45.96

STEP 2: Calculate the value of the items acquired in the exchange, which in this case, is the value of the sweaters.

3 × $15.50 = $46.50

STEP 3:

Calculate the difference between the value of the items acquired and the amount of money originally spent.

Value of the items acquired: 3 × $15.50 = $46.50

Amount of money originally spent: 2 × $22.98 = $45.96

Difference: (3 × $15.50) – (2 × $22.98)

24. The correct answer is C.

If you look at the answer choices, you will see that they are given in the nearest increments of 5.

So, we have to round the figures stated in the problem up or down to the nearest increment of 5.

104 on Monday is rounded to 105.

86 on Tuesday is rounded down to 85.

81 is rounded down to 80.

Then add these three figures together to get your result.

105 + 85 + 80 = 270

25. The correct answer is D.

We know that we have to round to the nearest hundredth.

The hundredth decimal place is the number 2 positions to the right of the decimal point.

For example, .01 is 1 one hundredth.

In our question, the first jump of 3.246 is rounded up to 3.25

The second jump of 3.331 is rounded down to 3.33

The third jump of 3.328 is rounded up to 3.33

Then add these three figures together to get your answer.

3.25 + 3.33 + 3.33 = 9.91

26. The correct answer is D.

You have to find the relationship between the number given in each row in the left column and the corresponding number in the right column. "9:50 am to 10:36 am" represents a journey time of 46 minutes.

11:15 to 12:01 is also 46 minutes, and so on.

If we go 46 minutes back from 5:51 pm, we arrive at 5:05 pm.

27. The correct answer is A.
We have the data set: 1.6, 2.9, 4.5, 2.5, 2.5, 5.1, 5.4
The median is the number that is in the middle of the data set.
So put the numbers in ascending order:
1.6, 2.5, 2.5, 2.9, 4.5, 5.1, 5.4
Then find the median or middle value:
1.6, 2.5, 2.5, **2.9**, 4.5, 5.1, 5.4

28. The correct answer is D.

The mode is the number in the set that occurs most frequently. Our data set is: 1050, 201, 1500, 700, 1242, 1500, 289, 957. The number 1500 is the only number that occurs more than once, so it is the mode.

29. The correct answer is A.

These are prime numbers in a series. Prime numbers are numbers which are only divisible by themselves and by 1. The next prime number after 11 is 13.

30. The correct answer is A.

Your first step is to calculate the total amount of items in the sample space:

4 red marbles + 6 green marbles + 10 white marbles = 20 marbles in total

The probability is expressed with the event in the numerator and the sample space in the denominator.

So, the chance of drawing a white marble is $^{10}/_{20} = ^1/_2$

ASVAB ARITHMETIC REASONING - PRACTICE TEST 4

1. Captain Smith needs to purchase rope for his fleet of yachts. He owns 26 yachts and needs 6 feet 10 inches of rope for each one. How much rope does he need in total?
    A. 152 feet
    B. 177 feet 8 inches
    C. 257 feet 8 inches
    D. 260 feet

2. Use the diagram below to answer the question that follows.

    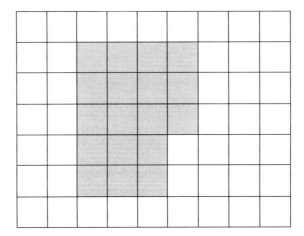

    Each square in the diagram above is one foot wide and one foot long. The gray area of the diagram represents the layout of New Town's water reservoir. What is the perimeter in feet of the reservoir?
    A. 16 feet
    B. 17 feet
    C. 18 feet
    D. 20 feet

3. During this term, Tom got the following scores on his math tests: 98, 78, 89, 85, and 90. What is the average of Tom's scores?
    A. 78
    B. 85
    C. 88
    D. 89

4. Use the table below to answer the question that follows.

Part	Total Number of Questions	Number of Questions Answered Correctly
1	15	12
2	25	20
3	35	32
4	45	32

Chantelle took a test that had four parts. The total number of questions on each part is given in the table above, as is the number of questions Chantelle answered correctly. What was Chantelle's percentage of correct answers for the entire test?
A. 75%
B. 80%
C. 86%
D. 90%

5.   Linda uses two bottles of ink every 5 days for her graphic design business. Approximately how many bottles of ink does she require for one month?
A.   12
B.   6
C.   5
D.   1

6.   Use the diagram below to answer the question that follows.

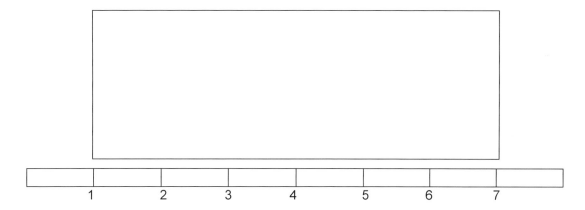

A scale drawing of a field is shown in the picture above. If the actual length of the field is 120 yards, what is the scale of the diagram?
A. 1 unit = 6 yards
B. 1 unit = 7 yards
C. 1 unit = 15 yards
D. 1 unit = 20 yards

7.   A photograph measures 4 inches by 6 inches. Tom wants to make a wooden frame for the photo. He needs an extra inch of wood at each of the four corners in order to finish off the edges. What total length of wood will he need in order to complete the project?
A. 10 inches
B. 12 inches
C. 24 inches
D. 36 inches

8.   It takes Mark 4 hours and 10 minutes to change the oil and filters in one car. At this rate, how long will it take him to do 12 cars?
     A. 40 hours
     B. 50 hours
     C. 56 hours
     D. 60 hours

9.   A company is making its budget for the cost of employees to attend conferences for the year. It costs $7,500 per year in total for the company plus C dollars per employee. During the year, the company has E employees. If the company has budgeted $65,000 for conference attendance, which equation can be used to calculate the maximum cost per employee?
     A. ($65,000 − $7,500) ÷ E
     B. ($65,000 − $7,500) ÷ C
     C. (C − $7,500) ÷ E
     D. $65,000 ÷ E

10. At an elementary school, 3 out of ten students are taking an art class. If the school has 650 students in total, how many total students are taking an art class?
     A.   65
     B. 130
     C. 195
     D. 217

11. Mrs. Emerson plays a card game with the children in her class. She has 12 cards that have a picture of a fish, 15 cards that have a picture of a dog, 25 cards that have a picture of a cat, and 18 cards that have picture of a rabbit. She draws cards from the deck at random and shows them to the class. If the first card she draws is a rabbit, what is the probability that the next card will be a cat or a rabbit? Note that once a card is drawn, it is removed from the deck.
     A. $^{25}/_{69}$
     B. $^{25}/_{70}$
     C. $^{42}/_{69}$
     D. $^{43}/_{69}$

12. A plumber charges $100 per job, plus $25 per hour worked. He is going to do 5 jobs this month. He will earn a total of $4,000. How many hours will he work this month? Please write your answer in the space provided.
     A. 140 hours
     B. 160 hours
     C. 180 hours
     D. 200 hours

13. Mount Arriba is 15,238 feet high. Mount Glacier is 9,427 feet high. Which of the following is the best estimate of the difference between the altitudes of the two mountains?
     A. 5,700
     B. 5,800
     C. 5,900
     D. 6,000

14. A construction company is building new homes on a housing development. It has an agreement with the municipality that *H* number of houses must be built every 30 days. If *H* number of houses are not built during the 30 day period, the company has to pay a penalty to the municipality of *P* dollars per house. The penalty is paid per house for the number of houses that fall short of the 30-day target. If *A* represents the actual number of houses built during the 30-day period, which equation below can be used to calculate the penalty for the 30-day period?
    A. $(H - P) \times 30$
    B. $(H - A) \times P$
    C. $(A - H) \times 30$
    D. $(A - H) \times P$

15. John is measuring plant growth as part of a botany experiment. Last week, his plant grew 7¾ inches, but this week his plant grew 10½ inches. What is the difference in growth in inches between the two weeks?
    A. 2¼ inches
    B. 2½ inches
    C. 2¾ inches
    D. 3¼ inches

16. At the beginning of a class, one-fourth of the students leave to attend band practice. Later, one half of the remaining students leave to go to PE. If there were 15 students remaining in the class at the end, how many students were in the class at the beginning?
    A. 30
    B. 40
    C. 45
    D. 50

17. In the last step of doing a calculation, Lee added 92 instead of subtracting 92. What shortcut can Lee perform in order to get the correct calculation?
    A. Add 92 to his erroneous result.
    B. Subtract 92 from his erroneous result.
    C. Add 184 to his erroneous result.
    D. Subtract 184 from his erroneous result.

18. Shaun is driving at 70 miles per hour. At 10:00 am, he sees this sign:

Washington	**140 miles**
Yorkville	**105 miles**
Zorster	**210 miles**

He continues driving at the same speed. Where will Shaun be at 11:00 am?
    A. 70 miles from Washington
    B. 105 miles from Washington
    C. 75 miles from Yorkville
    D. 80 miles from Yorkville

19. Maya spent the day counting cars for her job as a traffic controller. In the morning she counted 114 more cars than she did in the afternoon. If she counted 300 cars in total that day, how many cars did she count in the morning?
   A. 90
   B. 93
   C. 114
   D. 207

20. Shania is entering a talent competition which has three events. The third event (C) counts three times as much as the second event (B), and the second event counts twice as much as the first event (A). Which equation below can be used to calculate Shania's final score for the competition?
   A. A + 2B + C
   B. A + 2B + 3C
   C. A + 3B + 2C
   D. A + 2B + 6C

21. Tiffany buys five pairs of socks for $2.50 each. The next day, she decides to exchange these five pairs of socks for four different pairs that cost $3 each. She uses this equation to calculate her refund: $(5 \times \$2.50) - (4 \times \$3)$
   Which equation below could she have used instead?
   A. $(5 \times 4) - (3 \times 2.50)$
   B. $\$2.50 - 4(\$3 - \$2.50)$
   C. $(5 \times 4) + (3 \times 2.50)$
   D. $\$3 - (4 \times \$2.50)$

22. Mr. Carlson needs to calculate 35% of 90.
   To do so, he uses the following equation:
   $$\frac{35 \times 90}{100}$$
   Which of the following could he also have used?
   A. $(35 \times 90) \div 100$
   B. $(35 \div 90) \times 100$
   C. $(35 - 90) \times 100$
   D. $90 \times .0035$

23. Carl swam three races this week. The time of his first race was 36.21 seconds. The time of the second race was 35.78 seconds. The time of his third race was 34.93 seconds. If each of these times is rounded to the nearest one-tenth of a second, what is the estimate of Carl's total time for all three of the races?
   A. 106 seconds
   B. 106.8 seconds
   C. 106.9 seconds
   D. 107 seconds

24. Brooke drives 21 miles round trip every day between her home and her office. If her daily journey is rounded to the nearest 5 miles, which of the following is the best estimate of the total miles that Brooke drives in ten days?
   A. 150 miles
   B. 200 miles
   C. 210 miles
   D. 250 miles

25. Use the table below to answer the question that follows.

Waterloo Station Bus Timetable	
Departure Time	Arrival Time
9:18 am	11:06 am
10:32 am	12:20 pm
11:52 am	?
1:03 pm	2:51 pm

Bus journeys from Waterloo Station to a nearby town are always the same duration. What time is missing from the above timetable?
   A. 12:40 pm
   B. 1:34 pm
   C. 1:40 pm
   D. 1:48 pm

26. $5^8 \div 5^2 = ?$
   A. 25^6
   B. 25^4
   C. 5^6
   D. 5^4

27. $5! = ?$
   A. 120
   B. 50
   C. 25
   D. 20

28. What is the largest possible product of two even integers whose sum is 22?
   A. 120
   B. 100
   C. 44
   D. 11

29. In an athletic competition, the maximum possible amount of points was 25 points per participant. The scores for 15 different participants are displayed in the graph below. What was the median score for the 15 participants?

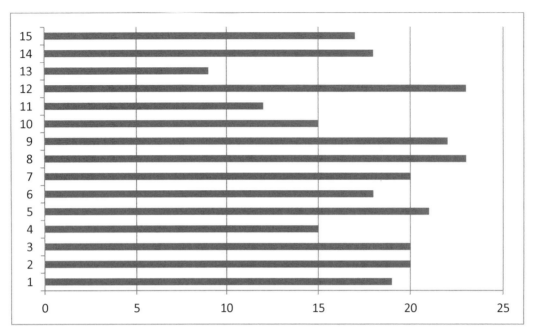

A. 8
B. 12
C. 13
D. 19

30. $\sqrt{16} \times |-5| = ?$
A. −80
B. −20
C. 11
D. 20

Practice Test 4 – Answers

1. B
2. C
3. C
4. B
5. A
6. D
7. C
8. B
9. A
10. C
11. C
12. A
13. B
14. B
15. C
16. B
17. D
18. A
19. D
20. D
21. B
22. A
23. C
24. B
25. C
26. C
27. A
28. A
29. D
30. D

Practice Test 4 – Explanations for the Answers

1. The correct answer is B.

He owns 26 yachts and needs 6 feet 10 inches of rope for each one.

Convert the feet and inches measurement to inches.

6 feet 10 inches =

(6 × 12) + 10 inches =

72 + 10 = 82 inches

Then multiply by the number of items.

26 × 82 = 2132 inches of rope needed

Then convert back to feet and inches.

2132 inches ÷ 12 = 177 feet 8 inches

2. The correct answer is C.

Count how many blocks lie along the outer edges of the shaded area in order to get your result.

Top boundary = 4 feet

Left side boundary = 5 feet

Bottom boundary = 3 feet

Right boundary = 6 feet (Don't forget to count the piece shaped like the upside-down "L" on the right.)

Then add these amounts to get your result.

4 + 5 + 3 + 6 = 18 feet

3. The correct answer is C.

To get the average, add up all of the items.

98 + 78 + 89 + 85 + 90 = 440

There are five scores, so there were five tests.

Divide the total points by the number of tests in order to get the average.

440 ÷ 5 = 88

4. The correct answer is B.

First of all, add up the number of questions answered correctly.

12 + 20 + 32 + 32 = 96

Then add up the total number of questions.

15 + 25 + 35 + 45 = 120

Now divide the number of questions answered correctly by the total number of questions to get her percentage score.

96 ÷ 120 = 80%

5. The correct answer is A.

Assuming there are 30 days in the month, we can divide as shown.

30 days ÷ 5 days per 2 bottles =

6 days × 2 bottles = 12 bottles needed for 1 month

6. The correct answer is D.

STEP 1: Determine the length of the field in units.

We can see that the right-hand side of the field is on the number 7. However, the field is not positioned over the left-hand side of the ruler.

So, the field is 6 units long.

STEP 2: Divide the actual length of the field by the units.

$120 \div 6 = 20$

STEP 3: Express the answer in units and yards.

1 unit = 20 yards

7. The correct answer is C.

Measure the length along the top and bottom of the frame, as well as the length of both sides in order to get the basic perimeter.

Top = 4 inches

Bottom = 4 inches

Left side = 6 inches

Right side = 6 inches

Total perimeter: 4 + 4 + 6 + 6 = 20 inches

Now add in the 4 extra inches for the four corners.

20 + 4 = 24 inches

8. The correct answer is B.

STEP 1: Convert into minutes the amount of time required to do one car.

4 hours and 10 minutes =

$(4 \times 60) + 10 =$

240 + 10 = 250 minutes needed to do one car

STEP 2: Multiply by the total output.

250 minutes × 12 cars = 3000 minutes

STEP 3: Convert the total amount of minutes back to hours and minutes

3000 minutes ÷ 60 = 50 hours

9. The correct answer is A.

The total amount of the budget is $65,000. The up-front cost is $7,500, so we can determine the remaining amount of available funds by deducting the up-front cost from the total: $65,000 − $7,500.

We have to divide the available amount by the number of employees (E) to get the maximum cost per employee: ($65,000 − $7,500) $\div E$

10. The correct answer is C.

Three out of ten students are taking the class. So, here we have the proportion:

$$\frac{3}{10} = \frac{?}{650}$$

STEP 1: Divide the total number of students by the denominator of the first fraction to get the number of groups.

650 ÷ 10 = 65 groups

STEP 2: Multiply the number of groups by the numerator of the first fraction in order to get the result.

3 × 65 = 195 art students

11. The correct answer is C.

Here is a more difficult probability question.

STEP 1: Remember that your first step is to determine the number of items in the sample space, before any items are removed.

Mrs. Emerson has 12 cards that have a picture of a fish, 15 cards that have a picture of a dog, 25 cards that have a picture of a cat, and 18 cards that have picture of a rabbit.

12 + 15 + 25 + 18 = 70

STEP 2: Determine the amount in the sample space after any items have been removed.

We know that the first card she draws is a rabbit, so she has taken one item from the sample space.

70 − 1 = 69

STEP 3: Determine the amount for the event.

Our event is cards with cats or rabbits. Before any items were removed, we had 25 cards with picture of a cat, and 18 cards with picture of a rabbit. Then one card with a rabbit was removed. So, add and subtract as shown.

25 + 18 − 1 = 42 cat or rabbit cards remaining

STEP 4: The probability is expressed as a fraction, with the event on the top and the sample space on the bottom.

$^{42}/_{69}$

12. The correct answer is A.

The plumber is going to earn $4,000 for the month. He charges a set fee of $100 per job, and he will do 5 jobs, so we can calculate the total set fees first: $100 set fee per job × 5 jobs = $500 total set fees. Then deduct the set fees from the total for the month in order to determine the total for the hourly pay: $4,000 − $500 = $3,500. He earns $25 per hour, so divide the hourly rate into the total hourly pay in order to determine the number of hours he will work:

$3,500 total hourly pay ÷ $25 per hour = 140 hours to work

13. The correct answer is B.

We have to subtract to find the difference in height between the two mountains.

First of all, round each number up or down.

Looking at the answer choices, we can see that we need to round to the nearest increment of 100.

15,238 is rounded down to 15,200

9,427 is rounded down to 9,400

Now subtract to get your answer.

15,200 − 9,400 = 5,800

14. The correct answer is B.

First, we need to calculate the shortage in the amount of houses actually built. If H represents the amount of houses that should be built and A represents the actual number of houses built, then the shortage is calculated as: $H − A$. The company has to pay P dollars per house for the shortage, so we calculate the total penalty by multiplying the shortage by the penalty per house: $(H − A) \times P$

15. The correct answer is C.

STEP 1: You can express the fractions as decimals for the sake of simplicity.

10½ = 10.50

7¾ = 7.75

STEP 2: Then subtract to find the increase.

10.50 − 7.75 = 2.75

STEP 3: Then convert back to a mixed number.

2.75 = 2¾

16. The correct answer is B.

One-fourth of the students leave to attend band practice. Later, one half of the remaining students leave to go to PE.

We know we have 15 students remaining in class after the others have left.

So, work backwards based on the facts given.

STEP 1: We have 15 students left after half of the students have left to go to PE, so divide 15 by one-half. So, if x represents the number of remaining students after the group of students has left for PE, we have the following equation.

$15 = x − (x × ½)$

$15 = x − ½ x$

$15 = ½ x$

$15 × 2 = ½ x × 2$

$30 = x$

So, there were 30 students in class before PE.

STEP 2: We have 30 students after ¼ of them have gone to band, so we have the following equation.

$30 = x − (x × ¼)$

$30 = x − ¼ x$

$30 = ¾ x$

$30 × 4 = ¾ x × 4$

$120 = 3x$

$120 ÷ 3 = 3x ÷ 3$

$40 = x$

So, there were 40 students in the class at the beginning.

17. The correct answer is D.

He needs to subtract the 92 that he added by mistake to get back to his starting point. Then he needs to subtract 92 again to get the correct result. So, he can subtract 92 two times or simply shortcut by subtracting 184 since 82 × 82 = 194.

18. The correct answer is A.

STEP 1: Determine the distance traveled.

If he is traveling 70 miles an hour, he will have traveled 70 miles after one hour has passed.

STEP 2: Determine the distance from the towns listed on the sign, considering that he has traveled for one hour.

Washington: 140 − 70 = 70 miles from Washington

Yorkville: 105 − 70 = 35 miles from Yorkville

Zorster: 210 − 70 = 140 miles from Zorster

STEP 3: Compare the above figures to your answer choices to get your result. After an hour, he is 70 miles from Washington, so A is correct.

19. The correct answer is D.

STEP 1: Subtract the excess from the total.

300 − 114 = 186

STEP 2: Allocate the difference into its respective parts.

We are dividing the day into two parts: morning and afternoon. There were 186 cars in total without the excess, so divide this into two parts.

186 ÷ 2 = 93

STEP 3: Determine the amount for the larger part.

There were 114 more cars in the morning, so add this back in.

93 + 114 = 207 cars in the morning

20. The correct answer is D.

Work out the equation based on the facts provided in the problem.

The second event (B) counts twice as much as the first event (A), so we need to represent the value of the second event as 2B.

The third event (C) counts three times as much as the second event, so we need to multiply the value of the second event by 3.

2 × 3 = 6

So, the value of the third event is 6C.

Therefore, the equation is A + 2B + 6C.

21. The correct answer is B.

Here is an exchange problem.

STEP 1: Think about the value of the four pairs of socks she is getting in the exchange. These socks cost 50 cents more each than the pairs she has already bought. So, we can express the difference in value of those four pairs of socks as: 4 × ($3 - $2.50)

STEP 2: Take into account the value of the extra pair of socks. She paid $2.50 for a fifth pair of socks, but she is only getting four pairs back on the exchange, so she is owed money back for that part of the purchase.

Therefore, we can calculate the refund owing as $2.50 − 4($3 - $2.50)

22. The correct answer is A.

The line in any fraction can be treated as the division symbol. Accordingly, we can divide by the denominator, which is 100 in this case.

$$\frac{35 \times 90}{100} = (35 \times 90) \div 100$$

23. The correct answer is C.

Remember that the tenth is the decimal just to the right of the decimal point.

So, we need to round as required.

The first race was 36.21 seconds, which is rounded down to 36.2

The second race was 35.78 seconds, which is rounded up to 35.8

The third race was 34.93 seconds, which is rounded down to 34.9

Now add these figures together.

36.2 + 35.8 + 34.9 = 106.9

24. The correct answer is B.

We round the daily distance to 20, and then multiply by 10 to get the estimate of 200.

25. The correct answer is C.

Each journey is 108 minutes (1 hour and 48 minutes) in duration.

So, we need to add 108 minutes to the departure time of 11:52 to get the arrival time of 1:40.

26. The correct answer is C.

If the base number is the same, and the problem asks you to divide, you subtract the exponents. $5^8 \div 5^2 = 5^{8-2} = 5^6$

27. The correct answer is A.

Remember to multiply the number provided by every lesser whole number.

$5! = (5 \times 4 \times 3 \times 2 \times 1) = (5 \times 4 \times 3 \times 2) = 120$

28. The correct answer is A.

For problems that ask you to find the largest possible product of two even integers, first you need to divide the sum by 2. The sum in this problem is 22, so we need to divide this by 2.

$22 \div 2 = 11$

Now take the result from this division and find the 2 nearest even integers that are 1 number higher and lower.

11 + 1 = 12

11 − 1 = 10

Then multiply these two numbers together in order to get the product.

12 × 10 = 120

29. The correct answer is D.

The median is the number that is halfway through the set.

Our data set is: 19, 20, 20, 15, 21, 18, 20, 23, 22, 15, 12, 23, 9, 18, 17.

First, put the numbers in ascending order:

9, 12, 15, 15, 17, 18, 18, 19, 20, 20, 20, 21, 22, 23, 23

We have 15 numbers, so the 8th number in the set is halfway and is therefore the median.

9, 12, 15, 15, 17, 18, 18, **19**, 20, 20, 20, 21, 22, 23, 23

30. The correct answer is D.

Determine the square root.

$\sqrt{16} = 4$

Then determine the absolute value

$|-5| = 5$

Then multiply to get your result

$4 \times 5 = 20$

ASVAB ARITHMETIC REASONING - PRACTICE TEST 5

1. The temperature on Saturday was 62° F at 5:00 pm and 38° F at 11:00 pm. If the temperature fell at a constant rate on Saturday, what was the temperature at 9:00 pm?
    A. 46° F
    B. 50° F
    C. 54° F
    D. 58° F

2. In the last step of doing a calculation, Adam subtracted 180 instead of adding 180. What number can Adam add to his final erroneous result in order to get the correct calculation?
    A.   90
    B. 180
    C. 270
    D. 360

3. A painter needs to paint 8 rooms, each of which have a surface area of 2000 square feet. If one bucket of paint covers 900 square feet, what is the fewest number of buckets of paint that must be used to complete all 8 rooms?
    A. 3
    B. 17
    C. 18
    D. 19

4. Susan jogged 3.6 miles in $^3/_4$ of an hour. What was her average jogging speed in miles per hour?
    A. 2.7
    B. 4.0
    C. 4.2
    D. 4.8

5. When 1523.48 is divided by 100, which digit of the resulting number is in the tenths place?
    A. 1
    B. 2
    C. 3
    D. 4

6. The ratio of males to females in the senior year class of Carson Heights High School was 6 to 7. If the total number of students in the class is 117, how many males are in the class?
    A. 48
    B. 54
    C. 56
    D. 58

7. The total funds, represented by variable F, available for P charity projects is represented by the equation F = $500P + $3,700. If the charity has $40,000 available for projects, what is the greatest number of projects that can be completed?
   A. 72
   B. 73
   C. 74
   D. 79

8. A cafeteria serves spaghetti to senior citizens on Fridays. The spaghetti comes prepared in large containers, and each container holds 15 servings of spaghetti. The cafeteria is expecting 82 senior citizens this Friday. What is the least number of containers of spaghetti that the cafeteria will need in order to serve all 82 people?
   A. 4
   B. 5
   C. 6
   D. 7

9. A caterpillar travels 10.5 inches in 45 seconds. How far will it travel in 6 minutes?
   A. 45 inches
   B. 63 inches
   C. 64 inches
   D. 84 inches

10. The Jones family needs to dig a new well. The well will be 525 feet deep, and it will be topped with a windmill which will be 95 feet in height. What is the distance from the deepest point of the well to the top of the windmill?
    A. 95 feet
    B. 430 feet
    C. 525 feet
    D. 620 feet

11. The ratio of bags of apples to bags of oranges in a particular grocery store is 2 to 3. If there are 44 bags of apples in the store, how many bags of oranges are there?
    A. 33
    B. 48
    C. 55
    D. 66

12. Al uses a jar of coffee every week. How many jars of coffee will he need to last the entire year?
    A. 48
    B. 50
    C. 52
    D. 53

13. At the beginning of class, $^1/_5$ of the students leave to go to singing lessons. Then $^1/_4$ of the remaining students leave to go to the principal's office. If 18 students are then left in the class, how many students were there at the beginning of class?

    A. 30
    B. 90
    C. 25
    D. 45

14. Patty works 23 hours a week at a part time job for which she receives $7.50 an hour. She then gets a raise, after which she earns $184 per week. She continues to work 23 hours per week. How much did her hourly pay increase?

    A. 50 cents an hour
    B. 75 cents an hour
    C. $1.00 an hour
    D. $8.00 an hour

15. A military academy had 300 students at the beginning of January. It lost 5% of its students during the month. However, 15 new students joined the academy on the last day of the month. If this pattern continues for the next two months, how many students will there be at the academy at the end of March?

    A. 285
    B. 300
    C. 310
    D. 315

16. A meal out for the entire family costs $85.97. If Dave gave the cashier $100, how much change will he get back?

    A. $4.03
    B. $5.03
    C. $14.03
    D. $15.03

17. A motorcycle traveled 38.4 miles in $^4/_5$ of an hour. What was the speed of the motorcycle in miles per hour?

    A. 9.6
    B. 30.72
    C. 48
    D. 52

18. A factory that makes microchips produces 20 times as many functioning chips as defective chips. If the factory produced 11,235 chips in total last week, how many of them were defective?

    A.   535
    B.   561
    C.   1,070
    D. 10,700

19. One hundred students took an English test. The 55 female students in the class had an average score of 87, while the 45 male students in the class had an average of 80. What is the average test score for all 100 students in the class?
   A. 82.00
   B. 83.15
   C. 83.50
   D. 83.85

20. Toby is going to buy a car. The total purchase price of the car, including interest, is represented by variable C. He will pay D dollars immediately, and then he will make equal payments (P) each month for a certain number of months (M). Which equation below represents the amount of his monthly payment (P)?

   A. $\frac{C-D}{M}$

   B. $\frac{C}{M} - D$

   C. $\frac{M}{C-D}$

   D. $D - \frac{C}{M}$

21. A group of friends are going on vacation. Person A's suitcase weighs $14^3/_4$ pounds. Person B's suitcase weighs $20^1/_5$ pounds. Person C's suitcase weighs 36.35 pounds. What is the total weight of all three suitcases?
   A. 70.475
   B. 71.05
   C. 71.15
   D. 71.30

22. Faith drove into town at a rate of 50 miles per hour. She shopped in town for 20 minutes, and then drove home on the same route at a rate of 60 miles per hour. Which of the following equations best expresses the total time (Tt) that it took Faith to make the journey and do the shopping? Note that the variable D represents the distance in miles from Faith's house to town.
   A. Tt + 20 minutes = 110 × D
   B. Tt + 20 minutes = [(50 + 60) ÷ 2] × D
   C. $Tt = [(D \div 50) + (D \div 60)] + 20 \text{ minutes}$
   D. $Tt = D \div 110$

23. A baseball team sells T-shirts and sweatpants to the public for a fundraising event. The total amount of money the team earned from these sales was $850. t represents the number of T-shirts sold and s represents the number of sweatpants sold. The total sales in dollars is represented by the equation $25t + 30s$. The amount earned by selling sweatpants is what fraction of the total amount earned?
   A. s/850
   B. 30s/850
   C. (25t + 30s)/850
   D. t/850

24. 2 inches on a scale drawing represents F feet. Which of the following equations represents $F + 1$ feet on the drawing?

A. $\frac{2(F+1)}{F}$

B. $\frac{(F+1)}{F}$

C. $\frac{2}{F+1}$

D. $\frac{2F}{F+1}$

25. The speed of light in a recent experiment was 300,000,000 meters per second. How far did the light travel in 100 seconds?

A. 3.0×10^{11} meters
B. 3.0×10^{12} meters
C. 3.0×10^{9} meters
D. 3.0×10^{10} meters

26. Mrs. Thompson is having a birthday party for her son. She is going to give balloons to the children. She has one bag that contains 13 balloons, another that contains 22 balloons, and a third that contains 25 balloons. If 12 children are going to attend the party including her son, and the total amount of balloons is to be divided equally among all of the children, how many balloons will each child receive?

A. 3
B. 4
C. 5
D. 6

27. A bookstore is offering a 15% discount on books. Janet's purchase would be $90 at the normal price. How much will she pay after the discount?

A. $75.50
B. $76.50
C. $77.50
D. $85.50

28. The price of a sofa at a local furniture store was x dollars on Wednesday this week. On Thursday, the price of the sofa was reduced by 10% of Wednesday's price. On Friday, the price of the sofa was reduced again by 15% of Thursday's price. Which of the following expressions can be used to calculate the price of the sofa on Friday?

A. $(0.25)x$
B. $(0.75)x$
C. $(0.10)(0.15)x$
D. $(0.90)(0.85)x$

29. There are three boys in a family, named Alex, Burt, and Zander. Alex is twice as old as Burt, and Burt is one year older than three times the age of Zander. Which of the following statements best describes the relationship between the ages of the boys?

A. Alex is 4 years older than 6 times the age of Zander.

B. Alex is 2 years older than 6 times the age of Zander.

C. Alex is 4 years older than 3 times the age of Zander.

D. Alex is 2 years older than 3 times the age of Zander.

30. A clothing store sells jackets and coats at a discount during a sales period. The total amount of money the store collected for sales of coats and jackets during the sales period was $4,000. The amount of money earned from selling jackets was one-third of that earned from selling coats. The coats sold for $20 each. How many coats did the store sell during the sales period?

A.   15

B.   20

C. 150

D. 200

Practice Test 5 – Answers

1. A
2. D
3. C
4. D
5. B
6. B
7. A
8. C
9. D
10. D
11. D
12. C
13. A
14. A
15. B
16. C
17. C
18. A
19. D
20. A
21. D
22. C
23. B
24. A
25. D
26. C
27. B
28. D
29. B
30. C

Practice Test 5 – Explanations for the Answers

1. The correct answer is A.

First of all, you need to determine the difference in temperature during the entire time period: 62 − 38 = 24 degrees less. Then calculate how much time has passed. From 5:00 PM to 11:00 pm, 6 hours have passed. Next, divide the temperature difference by the amount of time that has passed to get the temperature change per hour: 24 degrees ÷ 6 hours = 4 degrees less per hour. To calculate the temperature at the stated time, you need to calculate the time difference. From 5:00 pm to 9:00 pm, 4 hours have passed. So, the temperature difference during the stated time is 4 hours × 4 degrees per hour = 16 degrees less. Finally, deduct this from the beginning temperature to get your final answer.

62° F − 16° F = 46° F

2. The correct answer is D.

He subtracted 180 by mistake, so we need to add that back to correct the error. Then we need to add 180 for the original calculation that he should have done.

180 × 2 = 360

3. The correct answer is C.

This is a question that requires you to find the fewest multiples of an item. Be mindful of the words "fewest" and "greatest" in problems like this one, since it will normally be impossible to purchase a fractional part of the item in the question. Therefore, you will need to round your result up or down accordingly. For your first step, determine how many square feet there are in total: 2000 square feet per room × 8 rooms = 16,000 square feet in total

Then you need to divide by the coverage rate: 16,000 square feet to cover ÷ 900 square feet coverage per bucket = 17.77 buckets needed. It is not possible to purchase a partial bucket of paint, so 17.77 is rounded up to 18 buckets of paint.

4. The correct answer is D.

This problem involves the calculation of miles per hour. To solve the problem, divide the distance traveled by the time in order to get the speed in miles per hour.

Remember that in order to divide by a fraction, you need to invert the fraction, and then multiply.

$3.6 \text{ miles} \div {}^{3}/_{4} =$

$3.6 \times {}^{4}/_{3} =$

$(3.6 \times 4) \div 3 =$

$14.4 \div 3 = 4.8 \text{ miles per hour}$

5. The correct answer is B.

This question assesses your understanding of decimals. Remember that the number after the decimal is in the tenths place, the second number after the decimal is in the hundredths place, and the third number after the decimal is in the thousandths place.

Perform the division, and then check the decimal places of the numbers. Divide as follows: 1523.48 ÷ 100 = 15.2348

Reading our result from left to right: 1 is in the tens place, 5 is in the ones place, 2 is in the tenths place, 3 is in the hundredths place, 4 is in the thousandths place, and 8 is in the ten-thousandths place.

6. The correct answer is B.

A ratio can be expressed by using the word "to" or by separating the amounts in the subsets with a colon. So, our ratio is expressed as 6 to 7 or 6:7. For your first step, add the subsets of the ratio together: 6 + 7 = 13

Then divide this into the total: 117 ÷ 13 = 9

Finally, multiply the result from the previous step by the subset of males from the ratio: 6 × 9 = 54 males in the class

7. The correct answer is A.

The equation is: F = $500P + $3,700. We are told that the total funds are $40,000 so put that in the equation to solve the problem.

$40,000 = $500P + $3,700
$40,000 − $3,700 = $500P
$36,300 = $500P
$36,300 ÷ 500 = $500 ÷ 500P
$36,300 ÷ 500 = 72.6
Since a fraction of a project cannot be undertaken, the greatest number of projects is 72.

8. The correct answer is C.

Divide and then round up: 82 people in total ÷ 15 people served per container = 5.467 containers. We need to round up to 6 since we cannot purchase a fractional part of a container.

9. The correct answer is D.

The question is asking us about a time duration of 6 minutes, so we need to calculate the amount of seconds in 6 minutes: 6 minutes × 60 seconds per minute = 360 seconds in total. Then divide the total time by the amount of time needed to make one journey: 360 seconds ÷ 45 seconds per journey = 8 journeys. Finally, multiply the number of journeys by the amount of inches per journey in order to get the total inches: 10.5 inches for 1 journey × 8 journeys = 84 inches in total

10. The correct answer is D.

Add the feet above ground to the feet below ground to get the total distance.

525 + 95 = 620 feet

11. The correct answer is D.

The ratio of bags of apples to bags of oranges is 2 to 3, so for every two bags of apples, there are three bags of oranges. First, take the total amount of bags of apples and divide by 2: 44 ÷ 2 = 22. Then multiply this by 3 to determine how many bags of oranges are in the store: 22 × 3 = 66.

12. The correct answer is C.

If Al uses a jar of coffee every week, he needs 52 jars to last a year since there are 52 weeks in a year.

13. The correct answer is A.

Work backwards based on the facts given. There are 18 students left at the end after one-fourth of them left for the principal's office. So, set up an equation for this:

$18 + {}^{1}/_{4}T = T$
$18 + {}^{1}/_{4}T - {}^{1}/_{4}T = T - {}^{1}/_{4}T$
$18 = {}^{3}/_{4}T$
$18 × 4 = {}^{3}/_{4}T × 4$
$72 = 3T$
$72 ÷ 3 = 3T ÷ 3$

24 = T

So, before the group of pupils left to see the principal, there were 24 students in the class. We know that one-fifth of the students left at the beginning to go to singing lessons, so we need to set up an equation for this:

$24 + \frac{1}{5}T = T$

$24 + \frac{1}{5}T - \frac{1}{5}T = T - \frac{1}{5}T$

$24 = \frac{4}{5}T$

$24 \times 5 = \frac{4}{5}T \times 5$

$120 = 4T$

$120 \div 4 = 4T \div 4$

$30 = T$

14. The correct answer is A.

After her raise, she earns $184 per week. She continues to work 23 hours per week.

STEP 1: Determine the new hourly rate.

$184 ÷ 23 hours = $8 per hour

STEP 2: Determine the change in the hourly rate.

$8 - $7.50 = 50 cents per hour

15. The correct answer is B.

At the beginning of January, there are 300 students, but 5% of the students leave during the month, so we have 95% left at the end of the month: 300 × 95% = 285. Then 15 students join on the last day of the month, so we add that back in to get to the total at the end of January: 285 + 15 = 300. If this pattern continues, there will always be 300 students in the academy at the end of any month.

16. The correct answer is C.

The meal out cost $85.97, and Dave gave the cashier $100, so we need to subtract in order to determine how much change he will get. Put decimal points in the $100 to help guide you: $100.00 − $85.97 = $14.03

17. The correct answer is C.

Divide by the fractional hour in order to determine the speed for an entire hour:

38.4 miles ÷ $\frac{4}{5}$ of an hour = 38.4 × $\frac{5}{4}$ = (38 × 5) ÷ 4 = 48 mph

18. The correct answer is A.

The ratio of defective chips to functioning chips is 1 to 20. So, the defective chips form one group and the functioning chips form another group. Therefore, the total data set can be divided into groups of 21. Accordingly, $\frac{1}{21}$ of the chips will be defective. The factory produced 11,235 chips last week, so we calculate as follows: 11,235 × $\frac{1}{21}$ = 535

19. The correct answer is D.

STEP 1: First of all, you have to calculate the total amount of points earned by the entire class.

Multiply the female average by the amount of female students.

Total points for female students: 87 × 55 = 4785

Then multiply the male average by the amount of male students.

Total points for male students: 80 × 45 = 3600

STEP 2: Then add these two amounts together to find out the total points scored by the entire class.

Total points for entire class: 4785 + 3600 = 8385

STEP 3: When you have calculated the total amount of points for the entire class, you divide this by the total number of students in the class to get the class average. There are 100 total students in this class because there are 55 females and 45 males.

8385 ÷ 100 = 83.85

20. The correct answer is A.

Deduct the down payment from the purchase price, and then divide by the number of months to solve the problem. The total amount that Toby has to pay is represented by C. He is paying D dollars immediately, so we can determine the remaining amount that he owes by deducting his down payment from the total. So, the remaining amount owing is represented by the equation: C − D.

We have to divide the remaining amount owing by the number of months (M) to get the monthly payment: $P = (C - D) \div M = \frac{C-D}{M}$

21. The correct answer is D.

We have both fractions and decimals in this problem.

Convert the fractions in the mixed numbers to decimals.

$^3/_4 = 3 \div 4 = 0.75$

$^1/_5 = 1 \div 5 = 0.20$

Then represent the mixed numbers as decimal numbers.

Person 1: $14^3/_4 = 14.75$

Person 2: $20^1/_5 = 20.20$

Person 3: 36.35

Then add all three amounts together to find the total.

14.75 + 20.20 + 36.35 = 71.30

22. The correct answer is C.

In this problem, we need to calculate the time spent on a journey. Read the problem carefully to make sure that you have understood all of the required facts.

The amount of time in hours (T) multiplied by miles per hour (mph) gives us the distance traveled (D). So, the equation for distance traveled is:

$T \times mph = D$

The problem tells us that we need to calculate T, so we need to isolate T by changing our equation as follows:

$T \times mph = D$

$(T \times mph) \div mph = D \div mph$

$T = D \div mph$

In our problem, Faith drives home on the same route that she took into town, so we need to calculate the traveling time for the journey into town, as well as for the journey home:

$(D \div 50) + (D \div 60) = T$

Then add back the 20 minutes she spent in town to get the total time:

$Tt = [(D \div 50) + (D \div 60)] + 20 \text{ minutes}$

23. The correct answer is B.

We need to set up a fraction, the numerator of which consists of the amount of sales in dollars for sweatpants, and the denominator of which consists of the total amount of sales in dollars for both items. The problem tells us that the amount of sales in dollars for sweatpants is 30s and the total amount of sales is 850, so the answer is 30s/850.

24. The correct answer is A.

This question requires you to set up ratios for a scale drawing. Set up ratios for each of the measurements, and then cross multiply to solve. We know that 2 inches represents F feet. We can set this up as a ratio 2/F. Next, we need to calculate the ratio for F + 1. The number of inches that represents F + 1 is unknown, so we will refer to this unknown as x.

So we have:

$$\frac{2}{F} = \frac{x}{F + 1}$$

Now cross multiply.

$$\frac{2}{F} = \frac{x}{F + 1}$$

$$F \times x = 2 \times (F + 1)$$

$$Fx = 2(F + 1)$$

Then isolate x to solve.

$$Fx = 2(F + 1)$$

$$Fx \div F = [2(F + 1)] \div F$$

$$x = \frac{2(F + 1)}{F}$$

25. The correct answer is D.

This problem involves identifying an equivalent expression in scientific notation. Scientific notation means that you give the expression as the result of two products: one of which is between 1 and 10 and contains a decimal, and the other of which contains 10 to an exponential power. The exponent of the 10 is the number of places that the decimal point must be shifted in order to give the number in long form.

Be careful with your zeroes. We are taking 300,000,000 (8 zeroes) times 100 (two zeroes). The result is: 300,000,000 × 100 = 30,000,000,000 = 3.0 × 10,000,000,000 (ten zeroes). So, the answer is: 3.0 × 10^{10} meters

26. The correct answer is C.

STEP 1: Add the items together to get the total amount of items available.

13 + 22 + 25 = 60 balloons in total

STEP 2: Divide the amount of items available by the number of people.

60 ÷ 12 = 5

27. The correct answer is B.

STEP 1: Determine the value of the discount by multiplying the normal price by the percentage discount.

$90 × 15% = $13.50 discount

STEP 2: Subtract the value of the discount from the normal price to get the new price.

$90 − $13.50 = $76.50

28. The correct answer is D.

The original price of the sofa on Wednesday was x. On Thursday, the sofa was reduced by 10%, so the price on Thursday was 90% of x or 0.90x. On Friday, the sofa was reduced by a further 15%, so the price on Friday was 85% of the price on Thursday, so we can multiply Thursday's price by 0.85 to get our answer: (0.90)(0.85)x

29. The correct answer is B.

Assign a variable for the age of each boy. Alex = A, Burt = B, and Zander = Z.

Alex is twice as old as Burt, so A = 2B. Burt is one year older than three times the age of Zander, so B = 3Z + 1. Then substitute the value of B into the first equation.

A = 2B

A = 2(3Z + 1)

A = 6Z + 2

So, Alex is 2 years older than 6 times the age of Zander.

30. The correct answer is C.

If the amount earned from selling jackets was one-third that of selling coats, the ratio of jacket to coat sales was 1 to 3. So, we need to divide the total sales of $4,000 into $1,000 for jackets and $3,000 for coats. We can then solve as follows:

$3,000 in coats sales ÷ $20 each = 150 coats sold

Format of the ASVAB Mathematics Knowledge Test

The ASVAB Mathematics Knowledge Test contains twenty-five questions.

Algebra questions on the exam cover:
- operations with polynomials
- factoring polynomial expressions
- fractions containing rational and radical expressions
- inequalities
- laws of exponents
- multiple solutions
- solving problems by substitution and elimination
- solving problems for an unknown variable
- square roots and radicals
- systems of equations

Geometry problems on the test can cover coordinate geometry, as well as plane and solid geometry. You may therefore see geometry problems on:
- Calculating the slope of the line
- Determining the midpoint between two points
- Finding x and y intercepts
- Triangles
- Squares
- Rectangles
- Circles
- Cones, Cylinders, and Other 3-D Shapes
- Hybrid figures

The practice tests in this study guide simulate the kinds of questions you will see on the actual ASVAB exam.

1. $(3x - 2y)^2 = ?$
    A. $9x^2 + 4y^2$
    B. $9x^2 - 6xy^2 + 4y^2$
    C. $9x^2 - 12xy + 4y^2$
    D. $9x^2 + 12xy + 4y^2$

Multiplying Polynomials Using the FOIL Method:

Polynomials are algebraic expressions that contain integers, variables, and variables which are raised to whole-number positive exponents.

You will see many problems in this format on the test: $(x + y)(x + y)$. Use the FOIL method to solve these problems, multiplying the terms in the parentheses in this order:

First – Outside – Inside – Last

The correct answer is C.

When you see algebra questions like this one, use the FOIL method. Study the solution below, which highlights the order to carry out the operations on the terms.

$(3x - 2y)^2 = (3x - 2y)(3x - 2y)$

FIRST: The first terms in each set of parentheses are $3x$ and $3x$:

$(\textbf{3x} - 2y)(\textbf{3x} - 2y)$

$3x \times 3x = 9x^2$

OUTSIDE: The terms on the outside are $3x$ and $-2y$: $(\textbf{3x} - 2y)(3x - \textbf{2y})$

$3x \times -2y = -6xy$

INSIDE: The terms on the inside are $-2y$ and $3x$: $(3x - \textbf{2y})(\textbf{3x} - 2y)$

$-2y \times 3x = -6xy$

LAST: The last terms in each set are $-2y$ and $-2y$: $(3x - \textbf{2y})(3x - \textbf{2y})$

$-2y \times -2y = 4y^2$

All of these individual results are put together for your final answer to the question.

$9x^2 - 6xy - 6xy + 4y^2 =$
$9x^2 - 12xy + 4y^2$

2. $(x^2 - x - 6) \div (x - 3) = ?$
    A. $2x$
    B. $x - 2$
    C. $-x - 2$
    D. $x + 2$

Dividing Polynomials Using Long Division:

You can think of long division of the polynomial as reversing the FOIL operation. In other words, your result will generally be in one of the following formats:

(x + y) or (x − y)

The correct answer is D.

In order to solve this type of problem, you must do long division of the polynomial.

Remember that you are subtracting the terms when you perform each part of the long division, so you need to be careful with negatives.

$$\begin{array}{r} x + 2 \\ x - 3\overline{)x^2 - x - 6} \\ \underline{x^2 - 3x} \\ 2x - 6 \\ \underline{2x - 6} \\ 0 \end{array}$$

3. What is the value of the expression $4x^2 + 2xy - y^2$ when $x = 2$ and $y = -2$?

   A. 4
   B. 6
   C. 8
   D. 12

Substituting Values in Polynomial Expressions:

You may be asked to calculate the value of an expression by substituting its values. To solve these problems, put in the values for x and y and multiply. Then do the addition and subtraction.

The correct answer is A.

$4x^2 + 2xy - y^2 =$

$(4 \times 2^2) + (2 \times 2 \times -2) - (-2^2) =$

$(4 \times 2 \times 2) + (2 \times 2 \times -2) - (-2 \times -2) =$

$(4 \times 4) + (2 \times -4) - (4) =$

$16 + (-8) - 4 =$

$16 - 12 = 4$

4. Perform the operation: $(5ab - 6a)(3ab^3 - 4b^2 - 3a)$

   A. $15a^2b^4 - 20ab^3 - 15a^2b - 18a^2b^3 - 24ab^2 - 18a^2$
   B. $15a^2b^4 - 20ab^3 - 15a^2b - 18a^2b^3 + 24ab^2 + 18a^2$
   C. $15a^2b^4 - 20ab^3 - 15a^2b - 18a^2b^3 - 24ab^2 + 18a^2$
   D. $15ab^4 - 20ab^3 - 15a^2b - 18a^2b^3 + 24ab^2 + 18a^2$

Operations on Polynomials Containing Three Terms:

If you see polynomial expressions that have more than two terms inside each set of parentheses, remember to use the distributive property of multiplication to solve the problem.

The correct answer is B.

STEP 1: Apply the distributive property of multiplication by multiplying the first term in the first set of parentheses by all of the terms inside the second pair of parentheses.

Then multiply the second term from the first set of parentheses by all of the terms inside the second set of parentheses.

$(5ab - 6a)(3ab^3 - 4b^2 - 3a) =$

$(5ab \times 3ab^3) + (5ab \times -4b^2) + (5ab \times -3a) + (-6a \times 3ab^3) + (-6a \times -4b^2) + (-6a \times -3a)$

STEP 2: Add up the individual products in order to solve the problem.

$(5ab \times 3ab^3) + (5ab \times -4b^2) + (5ab \times -3a) + (-6a \times 3ab^3) + (-6a \times -4b^2) + (-6a \times -3a)$

$15a^2b^4 - 20ab^3 - 15a^2b - 18a^2b^3 + 24ab^2 + 18a^2$

To solve these types of problems, you will also need to understand basic exponent laws. We will look at exponents in more detail in the "Law of Exponents" section.

5. Factor the following: $2xy - 6x^2y + 4x^2y^2$
   A. $2xy(1 + 3x - 2xy)$
   B. $2xy(1 - 3x + 2xy)$
   C. $2xy(1 + 3x + 2xy)$
   D. $2xy(1 - 3x - 2xy)$

Factoring Polynomials:

Factoring means that you have to break down a polynomial into smaller parts. In order to factor an equation, you must figure out what variables are common to each term of the equation.

The correct answer is B.

Looking at this equation, we can see that each term contains x. We can also see that each term contains y.

So, first factor out xy.

$2xy - 6x^2y + 4x^2y^2 =$

$xy(2 - 6x + 4xy)$

Then, think about integers. We can see that all of the terms inside the parentheses are divisible by 2. Now let's factor out the 2. To do this, we divide each term inside the parentheses by 2.

$xy(2 - 6x + 4xy) =$

$2xy(1 - 3x + 2xy)$

6. $\dfrac{x + \dfrac{1}{5}}{\dfrac{1}{x}} = ?$

A. $x^2 + 5$

B. $\dfrac{x^3}{5}$

C. $x^2 + \dfrac{x}{5}$

D. $\dfrac{x + \dfrac{1}{5}}{x}$

Fractions Containing Fractions:

When you see fractions that contain fractions, remember to treat the denominator as the division sign. Then invert the second fraction and multiply.

The correct answer is C.

As stated above, the fraction can also be expressed as division.

$$\frac{x + \frac{1}{5}}{\frac{1}{x}} = \left(x + \frac{1}{5}\right) \div \frac{1}{x}$$

Then invert the second fraction and multiply the fractions.

In this case $\frac{1}{x}$ becomes $\frac{x}{1}$ when inverted, which is then simplified to x.

$$\left(x + \frac{1}{5}\right) \div \frac{1}{x} =$$

$$\left(x + \frac{1}{5}\right) \times x =$$

$$x^2 + \frac{x}{5}$$

7. $\dfrac{x^5}{x^2 - 6x} + \dfrac{5}{x} = ?$

A. $\dfrac{4 + x^6}{x^2 - 3x}$

B. $\dfrac{4x^2 - 16x}{x^7}$

C. $\dfrac{x^5 + 5x + 30}{x^2 - 6x}$

D. $\dfrac{x^5 + 5x - 30}{x^2 - 6x}$

Adding and Subtracting Fractions Containing Rational Expressions:
Rational expressions are math problems that contain algebraic terms. To add or subtract two fractions that contain rational expressions, you need to calculate the lowest common denominator, just like you would for any other problem with fractions.

The correct answer is D.
Find the lowest common denominator. Since x is common to both denominators, we can convert the denominator of the second fraction to the LCD by multiplying by $(x - 6)$.

$$\frac{x^5}{x^2 - 6x} + \frac{5}{x} =$$

$$\frac{x^5}{x^2-6x} + \left(\frac{5}{x} \times \frac{x-6}{x-6}\right) =$$

$$\frac{x^5}{x^2-6x} + \frac{5x-30}{x^2-6x} =$$

$$\frac{x^5+5x-30}{x^2-6x}$$

8. $\dfrac{2x^3}{5} \times \dfrac{4}{x^2} = ?$

A. $\dfrac{8x}{5}$

B. $\dfrac{5}{8x}$

C. $\dfrac{8}{5}$

D. $8x$

Multiplying Fractions Containing Rational Expressions:
To multiply fractions containing rational expressions, multiply the numerator of the first fraction by the numerator of the second fraction to get the new numerator. Then multiply the denominators.

The correct answer is A.

Multiply the numerator of the first fraction by the numerator of the second fraction. Then multiply the denominators.

$$\frac{2x^3}{5} \times \frac{4}{x^2} = \frac{2x^3 \times 4}{5 \times x^2} = \frac{8x^3}{5x^2}$$

Then factor the numerator and denominator.

As stated previously, we will discuss operations on exponents in more depth in the "Laws of Exponents" section of the study guide.

$$\frac{8x^3}{5x^2} = \frac{8x(x^2)}{5(x^2)}$$

Then we can cancel out x^2 to solve the problem.

$$\frac{8x(x^2)}{5(x^2)} = \frac{8x}{5}$$

9. $\dfrac{6x+6}{x^2} \div \dfrac{3x+3}{x^3} = ?$

A. $2x$

B. $6x$

C. $18x^3$

D. $\dfrac{3x+3}{x}$

Dividing Fractions Containing Rational Expressions:

In order to divide fractions that contain rational expressions, invert the second fraction and multiply. Then cancel out any common factors. Be sure to cancel out completely.

The correct answer is A.

The first step in solving the problem is to invert and multiply by the second fraction.

$$\frac{6x+6}{x^2} \div \frac{3x+3}{x^3} =$$

$$\frac{6x+6}{x^2} \times \frac{x^3}{3x+3} =$$

$$\frac{x^3(6x+6)}{x^2(3x+3)}$$

Then factor the numerator and denominator. $(x + 1)$ is common to both the numerator and the denominator, so we can factor that out.

$$\frac{x^3(6x+6)}{x^2(3x+3)} =$$

$$\frac{x^3 6(x+1)}{x^2 3(x+1)}$$

Now cancel out the $(x + 1)$.

$$\frac{x^3 6(x+1)}{x^2 3(x+1)} =$$

$$\frac{x^3 6}{x^2 3} =$$

$$\frac{6x^3}{3x^2}$$

Now factor out x^2 and cancel it out.

$$\frac{6x^3}{3x^2} =$$

$$\frac{6x \times x^2}{3x^2} =$$

$$\frac{6x}{3}$$

The numerator and denominator share the factor of 3, so cancel out further in order to get your final result.

$$\frac{6x}{3} =$$

$$\frac{3 \times 2 \times x}{3} = 2x$$

10. $40 - \dfrac{3x}{5} \geq 10$, then $x \leq$?

A. 15
B. 30
C. 40
D. 50

Inequalities:

When solving inequality problems, isolate integers before dealing with any fractions. Also remember that if you multiply an inequality by a negative number, you have to reverse the direction of the less than or greater than sign.

The correct answer is D.

Deal with the whole numbers on each side of the equation first.

$$40 - \frac{3x}{5} \geq 10$$

$$(40 - 40) - \frac{3x}{5} \geq 10 - 40$$

$$-\frac{3x}{5} \geq -30$$

Then deal with the fraction.

$$-\frac{3x}{5} \geq -30$$

$$\left(5 \times -\frac{3x}{5}\right) \geq -30 \times 5$$

$$-3x \geq -30 \times 5$$

$-3x \geq -150$

Then deal with the remaining whole numbers.
$-3x \geq -150$
$-3x \div 3 \geq -150 \div 3$
$-x \geq -150 \div 3$
$-x \geq -50$
Then deal with the negative number.
$-x \geq -50$
$-x + 50 \geq -50 + 50$
$-x + 50 \geq 0$
Finally, isolate the unknown variable as a positive number.
$-x + 50 \geq 0$
$-x + x + 50 \geq 0 + x$
$50 \geq x$
$x \leq 50$

11. During the year, a scheduled flight with an international airline travels 9×10^2 miles per hour for 3×10^2 hours. How far has this flight traveled this year?
    A.   135,000 miles
    B.   270,000 miles
    C.   900,000 miles
    D. 1,350,000 miles

Laws of Exponents:
When the base numbers or variables are the same and you need to multiply, you add the exponents.
When the base numbers or variables are the same and you need to divide, you subtract the exponents.
For multiplication:
$$x^3 \times x^2 = x^5$$
For division:
$$x^3 \div x^2 = x^1 = x$$

The correct answer is B.
We need to multiply, so you add the exponents.
In this problem, we have to multiply the miles per hour times the number of hours in order to calculate the distance traveled. Since we have the base number of 10 for each number that has an exponent, we can add the exponents.
$(9 \times 10^2$ miles per hour$) \times (3 \times 10^2$ hours$) =$
$9 \times 3 \times 10^{(2 + 2)} =$
$9 \times 3 \times 10^4 =$
$9 \times 3 \times 10,000 = 270,000$ miles

12. An owner of a carnival attraction draws teddy bears out of a bag at random to give to prize winners. She has 10 brown teddy bears, 8 white teddy bears, 4 black teddy bears, and 2 pink teddy bears when she opens the attraction at the start of the day. The first prize winner of the day receives a brown teddy bear. What is the probability that the second prize winner will receive a pink teddy bear?

A. $^1/_{24}$

B. $^1/_{23}$

C. $^2/_{24}$

D. $^2/_{23}$

Probability – Advanced Problems:

You may see problems on basic probability on the ASVAB Arithmetic Reasoning test. However, advanced problems on probability may be included on the ASVAB Mathematics Knowledge Test. Advanced problems on probability usually require four steps.

STEP 1: Calculate how many items there are in total in the data set, which is also called the "sample space" or (S).

STEP 2: Reduce the data set if further items are removed.

STEP 3: Determine the chance of the event or desired outcome. You can determine the chance of the event by calculating how many items are available in the subset of the desired outcome.

STEP 4: State the result as a probability. Probability can be expressed as a fraction. The number of items available in the total data set at the time of the draw goes in the denominator. The chance of the desired outcome, which is also referred to as the event or (E), goes in the numerator of the fraction.

$$P = \frac{E}{S}$$

The correct answer is D.

You need to determine the amount of possible outcomes at the start of the day first of all.

The owner has 10 brown teddy bears, 8 white teddy bears, 4 black teddy bears, and 2 pink teddy bears when she opens the attraction at the start of the day. So, at the start of the day, she has 24 teddy bears: $10 + 8 + 4 + 2 = 24$

Then you need to reduce this amount by the quantity of items that have been removed. The problem tells us that she has given out a brown teddy bear, so there are 23 teddy bears left in the sample space: $24 - 1 = 23$

The event is the chance of the selection of a pink teddy bear. We know that there are two pink teddy bears left after the first prize winner receives his or her prize.

Finally, we need to put the event (the number representing the chance of the desired outcome) in the numerator and the number of possible remaining combinations (the sample space) in the denominator.

So the answer is $^2/_{23}$.

Reciprocals:

To find a reciprocal for a whole number, you need to express the reciprocal as a fraction, with 1 in the numerator and the whole number in the denominator.

To find a reciprocal for an algebraic expression, you need to express the reciprocal as a fraction, with 1 in the numerator and the algebraic expression in the denominator.

To find a reciprocal for a fraction, you need to change the position of the numerator and a denominator.

Look at the following examples.

The reciprocal of 8 is $^1/_8$.

The reciprocal of $x + y$ is $^1/_{x+y}$

The reciprocal of $^3/_4$ is $^4/_3$.

13. Solve the following by elimination.

$x + 4y = 30$

$2x + 2y = 36$

A. $x = 2$ and $y = 7$

B. $x = 4$ and $y = 14$

C. $x = 14$ and $y = 4$

D. $x = 16$ and $y = 2$

Solving by Elimination:

When you have to solve a problem by elimination, you will see two equations as in the following question. In order to solve by elimination, you need to subtract the second equation from the first equation.

The correct answer is C.

Look at the x term of the second equation, which is $2x$.

So, in order to eliminate the x variable, we need to multiply the first equation by 2 and then subtract the second equation from this result.

$x + 4y = 30$

$(2 \times x) + (2 \times 4y) = (30 \times 2)$

$2x + 8y = 60$

Now subtract the two equations.

$$2x + 8y = 60$$
$$-(2x + 2y = 36)$$
$$\overline{6y = 24}$$

Then solve for y.

$6y = 24$

$6y \div 6 = 24 \div 6$

$y = 4$

Using our first equation $x + 4y = 30$, substitute the value of 4 for y to solve for x.

$x + 4y = 30$

$x + (4 \times 4) = 30$

$x + 16 = 30$

$x + 16 - 16 = 30 - 16$

$x = 14$

14. If $3x - 2(x + 5) = -8$, then $x = ?$

A. 1

B. 2

C. 3

D. 5

The correct answer is B.
To solve this type of problem, do multiplication on the items in parentheses first.
$3x − 2(x + 5) = −8$
$3x − 2x − 10 = −8$
Then deal with the integers by putting them on one side of the equation.
$3x − 2x − 10 = −8$
$3x − 2x − 10 + 10 = −8 + 10$
$3x − 2x = 2$
Then solve for *x*.
$3x − 2x = 2$
$1x = 2$
$x = 2$

15. Express as a rational number: $\sqrt[3]{64}$
   A. 1
   B. 4
   C. 5
   D. 125

Square Roots, Cube Roots, and Other Radicals:
Square roots and cube roots are sometimes referred to as radicals.
"Rationalize" means that you have to perform the necessary mathematical operations in order to remove the square root symbol. This normally involves factoring in order to find square or cube roots.

The correct answer is B.
In this problem, you have to find the cube root in order to eliminate the radical.
Remember that the cube root is the number which satisfies the equation when multiplied by itself two times.
$$\sqrt[3]{64} = \sqrt[3]{4 \times 4 \times 4} = 4 = 4$$
Remember that the above question could also be worded as follows: What is the cube root of 64?

16. Consider the isosceles triangle in the diagram below.

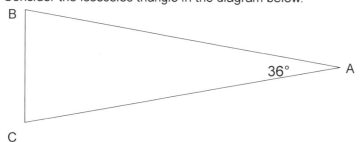

What is the measurement of ∠B?

A. 36°

B. 45°

C. 72°

D. 144°

Angles and Triangles:

Remember these principles on angles and triangles for your exam:

The sum of all three angles in any triangle must be equal to 180 degrees.

An isosceles triangle has two equal sides and two equal angles.

An equilateral triangle has three equal sides and three equal angles.

Angles that have the same measurement in degrees are called congruent angles.

Equilateral triangles are sometimes called congruent triangles.

Two angles are supplementary if they add up to 180 degrees. This means that when the two angles are placed together, they will form a straight line on one side.

Two angles are complementary (sometimes called adjacent angles) if they add up to 90 degrees. This means that the two angles will form a right triangle.

When two parallel lines are cut by a transversal (a straight line that runs through both of the parallel lines), 4 pairs of opposite (non-adjacent) angles are formed and 4 pairs of corresponding angles are formed. The opposite angles will be equal in measure, and the corresponding angles will also be equal in measure.

A parallelogram is a four-sided figure in which opposite sides are parallel and equal in length. Each angle will have the same measurement as the angle opposite to it, so a parallelogram has two pairs of opposite angles.

The sides of a 30° - 60° - 90° triangle are in the ratio of 1: $\sqrt{3}$: 2.

The correct answer is C.

The sum of all three angles in a triangle must be equal to 180 degrees, so we need to deduct the degrees given from 180° to find out the total degrees of the two other angles: 180° − 36° = 144°

Since the triangle is isosceles, the other two angles are equal in measure. Now divide this result by two in order to find out how many degrees each angle has.

144° ÷ 2 = 72°

17. In the figure below, XY is 4 inches long and XZ is 5 inches long.

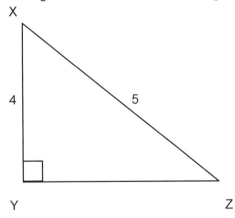

What is the area of triangle XYZ?

A. 3
B. 5
C. 6
D. 10

Area:

You will need to calculate the area of geometric shapes, such as circles, squares, triangles, and rectangles for the test.

Be sure that you know the following formulas from memory for the exam.

Area of a circle: $\pi \times r^2$ (radius squared)

Area of a square or rectangle: length × width

Area of a triangle: (base × height) ÷ 2

The correct answer is C.

In order to calculate the area of a triangle, you need this formula:

triangle area = (base × height) ÷ 2

However, the base length of the triangle described in the problem, which is line segment YZ, is not given. So, we need to calculate the base length using the Pythagorean theorem. We will look at the Pythagorean theorem again in the "Hypotenuse Length" section of the study guide.

We will state briefly here that according to the Pythagorean theorem, the length of the hypotenuse is equal to the square root of the sum of the squares of the two other sides.

$$\sqrt{4^2 + base^2} = 5$$

$$\sqrt{16 + base^2} = 5$$

Now square each side of the equation in order to solve for the base length.

$$\sqrt{16 + base^2} = 5$$

$$\left(\sqrt{16 + base^2}\right)^2 = 5^2$$

$16 + base^2 = 25$

$16 - 16 + base^2 = 25 - 16$

$base^2 = 9$

$$\sqrt{base^2} = \sqrt{9}$$

$base = 3$

Now solve for the area of the triangle.

triangle area = (base × height) ÷ 2

triangle area = (3 × 4) ÷ 2

triangle area = 12 ÷ 2

triangle area = 6

18.	If a circle has a diameter of 12, what is the circumference of the circle?
  	A.	6π
  	B.	12π
  	C.	24π
  	D.	36π

Circumference:
The formula for the circumference of a circle is: π × diameter
Diameter = radius × 2

The correct answer is B.
Substitute the value into the formula.
circumference = diameter × π
circumference = 12π
Remember not to confuse the formula for the circumference of a circle with the formula for the area of a circle.
circle area = radius^2 × π

19.	If a circle with center (−6, 6) is tangent to the x axis in the standard (x, y) coordinate plane, what is the diameter of the circle?
  	A.	−6
  	B.	−12
  	C.	 6
  	D.	 12

Diameter and Radius:
Diameter is the measurement across the entire width of a circle. Remember that diameter is always double the radius.

The correct answer is D.
If the center of a circle (x, y) is tangent to the x axis, then both of the following conditions are true:
(1) The point of tangency is equal to (x, 0).
(2) The distance between (x, y) and (x, 0) is equal to the radius.
The center of this circle is (−6, 6) and the point of tangency is (−6, 0).
So, we need to subtract these two coordinates in order to find the length of the radius.
(−6, 6) − (−6, 0) = (0, 6)
In other words, the radius length is 6, so the diameter length is 12.

20.	If one leg of a triangle is 5cm and the other leg is 12cm, what is the measurement of the hypotenuse of the triangle?
  	A.	$5\sqrt{12}$ cm
  	B.	$12\sqrt{5}$ cm
  	C.	$\sqrt{17}$ cm
  	D.	13 cm

The correct answer is D.
Substitute the values into the formula in order to find the solution for this problem:

$$\sqrt{A^2 + B^2} = C$$
$$\sqrt{5^2 + 12^2} = C$$
$$\sqrt{25 + 144} = C$$
$$\sqrt{169} = C$$

13 cm

21. Consider two stores in a town. The first store is a grocery store. The second is a pizza place where customers collect their pizzas. The grocery store is represented by the coordinates (−4, 2) and the pizza place is represented by the coordinates (2, −4). If the grocery store and the pizza place are connected by a line segment, what is the midpoint of this line?
A. (1, 1)
B. (−1, −1)
C. (2, 2)
D. (−2, −2)

The correct answer is B.
To find midpoints, you need to use these formulas:
midpoint $x = (x_1 + x_2) \div 2$
midpoint $y = (y_1 + y_2) \div 2$
First, find the midpoint of the x coordinates for (**−4**, 2) and (**2**, −4).
midpoint $x = (x_1 + x_2) \div 2$
midpoint $x = (−4 + 2) \div 2$
midpoint $x = −2 \div 2$
midpoint $x = −1$
Then find the midpoint of the y coordinates for (−4, **2**) and (2, **−4**).
midpoint $y = (y_1 + y_2) \div 2$
midpoint $y = (2 + −4) \div 2$
midpoint $y = −2 \div 2$
midpoint $y = −1$
So, the midpoint is (−1, −1)

22. What is the perimeter of a rectangle that has a length of 5 and a width of 3?
    A. 15
    B. 16
    C. 18
    D. 40

Perimeter of squares and rectangles:

The perimeter is the measurement along the outer side of a square, rectangle, or hybrid shape. You may see basic problems on perimeter on the Arithmetic Reasoning Test. However, you may see advanced problems on perimeter on the Mathematics Knowledge Test. In order to calculate the perimeter of squares and rectangles, you need to use the perimeter formula, which is provided below.

Perimeter = (length × 2) + (width × 2)

The correct answer is B.
Write out the formula.
(length × 2) + (width × 2)
Then substitute the values.
(5 × 2) + (3 × 2)
10 + 6 = 16

23. Marta runs up and down a hill near her house. The measurements of the hill can be placed on a two dimensional linear graph on which $x = 5$ and $y = 165$. If the line crosses the y axis at 15, what is the slope of this hill?
    A. 10
    B. 20
    C. 30
    D. 36

Slope and Slope-Intercept:

To put it in simple language, slope is the measurement of how steep a straight line on a graph is. Slope is represented by variable m.

The slope formula is as follows: $m = \dfrac{y_2 - y_1}{x_2 - x_1}$

In the slope-intercept formula, m is the slope, b is the y intercept (the point at which the line crosses the y axis), and x and y are points on the graph.

The slope-intercept formula is: $y = mx + b$

The correct answer is C.
Substitute the values into the formula.
$y = mx + b$
$165 = m5 + 15$
$165 - 15 = m5 + 15 - 15$
$150 = m5$
$150 \div 5 = m5 \div 5$
$30 = m$

24. Consider a cone with a height of 12 inches and a radius at its base of 3 inches. What is the volume of this cone?

   A. 3π

   B. 12π

   C. 36π

   D. 72π

Volume:

The test will have questions that ask you to calculate the volume of certain geometric shapes. You may need to calculate the volume of a cylinder, cone, or box on the examination.

Box volume: volume = base × width × height

Cone volume: (π × radius^2 × height) ÷ 3

Cylinder volume: π × radius^2 × height

The correct answer is C.

Substitute the values from the problem into the formula.

cone volume = [height × radius^2 × π] ÷ 3

cone volume = [12 × 3^2 × π] ÷ 3

cone volume = 36π

25. Find the x and y intercepts of the following equation: $x^2 + 4y^2 = 64$

   A. (8, 0) and (0, 4)

   B. (0, 8) and (4, 0)

   C. (4, 0) and (0, 8)

   D. (0, 4) and (8, 0)

---

x and y intercepts:

You may also be asked to calculate x and y intercepts in plane geometry problems.

The x intercept is the point at which a line crosses the x axis of a graph.

In order for the line to cross the x axis, y must be equal to zero at that particular point of the graph.

On the other hand, the y intercept is the point at which the line crosses the y axis.

So, in order for the line to cross the y axis, x must be equal to zero at that particular point of the graph.

For questions about x and y intercepts, substitute 0 for y in the equation provided. Then substitute 0 for x to solve the problem.

The correct answer is A.

Remember to substitute 0 for y in order to find the x intercept.

$x^2 + 4y^2 = 64$

$x^2 + (4 \times 0) = 64$

$x^2 + 0 = 64$

$x^2 = 64$

$x = 8$

Then substitute 0 for x in order to find the y intercept.

$x^2 + 4y^2 = 64$

$(0 \times 0) + 4y^2 = 64$

$0 + 4y^2 = 64$

$4y^2 \div 4 = 64 \div 4$

$y^2 = 16$

$y = 4$

So, the y intercept is $(0, 4)$ and the x intercept is $(8, 0)$.

ASVAB MATHEMATICS KNOWLEDGE - PRACTICE TEST 2

In order to simulate exam conditions, you should allow twenty-four minutes to take each practice test.

1. $(x^2 - 4) \div (x + 2) = ?$
   A. $x + 2$
   B. $x - 2$
   C. $x + 2x^2$
   D. $x - x^2$

2. If $5x - 2(x + 3) = 0$, then $x = ?$
   A. -2
   B. -1
   C. 1
   D. 2

3. Simplify the following equation: $(x + 3y)^2$
   A. $2(x - 3y)$
   B. $2x + 6y$
   C. $x^2 + 6xy + 9y^2$
   D. $x^2 + 6xy - 9y^2$

4. $(x + 3y)(x - y) = ?$
   A. $x^2 + 2xy - 3y^2$
   B. $2x + 2xy - 2y$
   C. $x^2 - 2xy + 3y^2$
   D. $2x - 2xy + 2y$

5. Evaluate the expression $6x^2 - xy + y^2$ if $x = 5$ and $y = -1$.
   A. 36
   B. 144
   C. 146
   D. 156

6. $x^2 + xy - y = 41$ and $x = 5$. What is the value of y?
   A. 2.6
   B. 4
   C. 6
   D. -4

7. $20 - \dfrac{3x}{4} \geq 17$, then $x \leq ?$
   A. -12
   B. -4
   C. -3
   D. 4

8. Factor: $18x^2 - 2x$
   A. $2x(9x - 1)$
   B. $9x(2x - 1)$
   C. $2x(9x - x)$
   D. $9x(2x - x)$

9. Simplify the following: $(5x^2 + 3x - 4) - (6x^2 - 5x + 8)$
   A. $-x^2 - 2x + 4$
   B. $-x^2 - 2x - 12$
   C. $-x^2 + 8x + 4$
   D. $-x^2 + 8x - 12$

10. $(x - 4)(3x + 2) = ?$
    A. $3x^2 - 10x - 8$
    B. $3x^2 - 10x + 8$
    C. $3x^2 + 14x - 8$
    D. $3x^2 + 14x + 8$

11. Factor the following: $x^2 + x - 20$
    A. $x(x - 1) - 20$
    B. $(x - 5)(x - 4)$
    C. $(x - 5)(x + 4)$
    D. $(x + 5)(x - 4)$

12. $(x - 4y)^2 = ?$
    A. $x^2 + 16y^2$
    B. $x^2 - 8xy - 16y^2$
    C. $x^2 - 8xy + 16y^2$
    D. $x^2 + 8xy - 16y^2$

13. If $4x - 3(x + 2) = -3$, then $x = ?$
    A. 9
    B. 3
    C. 1
    D. -3

14. $(x^2 - x - 12) \div (x - 4) = ?$
    A. $(x + 3)$
    B. $(x - 3)$
    C. $(-x + 3)$
    D. $(-x - 3)$

15. $\sqrt{6} \times \sqrt{5} = ?$
    A. $\sqrt{30}$
    B. $\sqrt{11}$

C. $6\sqrt{5}$

D. $5\sqrt{6}$

16. In the figure below, the circle centered at B is internally tangent to the circle centered at A. The length of line segment AB, which represents the radius of circle A, is 3 units and the smaller circle passes through the center of the larger circle. If the area of the smaller circle is removed from the larger circle, what is the remaining area of the larger circle?

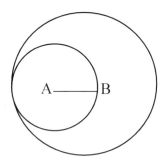

A. 3π

B. 6π

C. 9π

D. 27π

17. The perimeter of the square shown below is 24 units. What is the length of line segment AB?

A

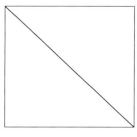

B

A. $\sqrt{24}$

B. $\sqrt{36}$

C. $\sqrt{72}$

D. 6

18. If a circle has a radius of 4, what is the circumference of the circle?

A. $\pi/8$

B. $\pi/16$

C. 8π

D. 16π

19. If a circle has a radius of 6, what is the area of the circle?
    A. 6π
    B. 12π
    C. 24π
    D. 36π

20. Find the midpoint between the following coordinates: (2, 2) and (4, –6)
    A. (3,4)
    B. (3,–2)
    C. (3,2)
    D. (3,–4)

21. A rectangular box has a base that is 5 inches wide and 6 inches long. The height of the box is 10 inches. What is the volume of the box?
    A. 30
    B. 110
    C. 150
    D. 300

22. Consider a right-angled triangle, where side M and side N form the right angle, and side L is the hypotenuse. If M = 3 and N = 2, what is the length of side L?
    A. 5
    B. $\sqrt{5}$
    C. 13
    D. $\sqrt{13}$

23. A magician pulls colored scarves out of a hat at random. The hat contains 5 red scarves and 6 blue scarves. The other scarves in the hat are green. If a scarf is pulled out of the hat at random, the probability that the scarf is red is $^1/_3$. How many green scarves are in the hat?
    A. 3
    B. 4
    C. 5
    D. 6

24. Which of the following statements best describes supplementary angles?
    A. Supplementary angles must add up to 90 degrees.
    B. Supplementary angles must add up to 180 degrees.
    C. Supplementary angles must add up to 360 degrees.
    D. Supplementary angles must be congruent angles.

25.	The diagram below shows a figure made from a semicircle, a rectangle, and an equilateral triangle. The rectangle has a length of 18 inches and a width of 10 inches. What is the perimeter of the figure?

A.	56 inches + 5π inches
B.	56 inches + 10π inches
C.	56 inches + 12.5π inches
D.	56 inches + 25π inches

Practice Test 2 – Answers

1. B

2. D

3. C

4. A

5. D

6. B

7. D

8. A

9. D

10. A

11. D

12. C

13. B

14. A

15. A

16. D

17. C

18. C

19. D

20. B

21. D

22. D

23. B

24. B

25. A

Practice Test 2 – Explanations for the Answers

1. The correct answer is B.

Our problem was $(x^2 - 4) \div (x + 2) = ?$

First, look at the integers in the equation. In this problem the integers are –4 and 2.

We know that we have to divide –4 by 2 because the dividend is $(x + 2)$.

$-4 \div 2 = -2$

We also know that we have to divide x^2 by x, because these are the first terms in each set of parentheses.

$x^2 \div x = x$

Now combine the two parts.

$-2 + x = x - 2$

Check your result by doing long division of the polynomial.

$$
\begin{array}{r}
x - 2 \\
x + 2 \overline{)x^2 \quad\ - 4} \\
\underline{x^2 + 2x} \\
-2x - 4 \\
\underline{-2x - 4} \\
0
\end{array}
$$

2. The correct answer is D.

To solve this type of problem, do the multiplication on the items in parentheses first.

$5x - 2(x + 3) = 0$

$5x - 2x - 6 = 0$

Then deal with the integers by putting them on one side of the equation as follows:

$5x - 2x - 6 + 6 = 0 + 6$

$3x = 6$

Then solve for x.

$3x = 6$

$x = 6 \div 3$

$x = 2$

3. The correct answer is C.

This type of algebraic expression is known as a polynomial. When multiplying polynomials, you should use the FOIL method. This means that you multiply the terms two at a time from each of the two parts of the equation in this order:

First – Outside – Inside – Last

$(x + 3y)^2 = (x + 3y)(x + 3y)$

FIRST – Multiply the first term from the first set of parentheses with the first term from the second set of parentheses.

$(\boldsymbol{x} + 3y)(\boldsymbol{x} + 3y)$

$x \times x = x^2$

OUTSIDE – Multiply the first term from the first set of parentheses with the second term from the second set of parentheses.

$(\boldsymbol{x} + 3y)(x + \boldsymbol{3y})$

$x \times 3y = 3xy$

INSIDE – Multiply the second term from the first set of parentheses with the first term from the second set of parentheses.

$(x + \boldsymbol{3y})(\boldsymbol{x} + 3y)$

$3y \times x = 3xy$

LAST– Multiply the second term from the first set of parentheses with the second term from the second set of parentheses.

$(x + \boldsymbol{3y})(x + \boldsymbol{3y})$

$3y \times 3y = 9y^2$

Then we add all of the above products together to get the answer.

$x^2 + 3xy + 3xy + 9y^2 =$

$x^2 + 6xy + 9y^2$

4. The correct answer is A.

Remember to use the FOIL method when you multiply. As you will see below, if a term or variable is subtracted within the parentheses, you have to keep the negative sign with it when you multiply.

FIRST: $(\boldsymbol{x} + 3y)(\boldsymbol{x} - y)$

$x \times x = x^2$

OUTSIDE: $(\boldsymbol{x} + 3y)(x - \boldsymbol{y})$

$x \times -y = -xy$

INSIDE: $(x + \boldsymbol{3y})(\boldsymbol{x} - y)$

$3y \times x = 3xy$

LAST: $(x + \boldsymbol{3y})(x - \boldsymbol{y})$

$3y \times -y = -3y^2$

Then add all of the above once you have completed FOIL.

$x^2 - xy + 3xy - 3y^2 =$

$x^2 + 2xy - 3y^2$

5. The correct answer is D.

"Evaluate" means to solve. So, to solve this problem, put in the values for x and y and multiply. Remember that two negatives together make a positive and to be careful when multiplying negative numbers.

$6x^2 - xy + y^2 =$

$(6 \times 5^2) - (5 \times -1) + (-1^2) =$

$(6 \times 5 \times 5) - (-5) + 1 =$

$(6 \times 25) + 5 + 1 =$

$150 + 5 + 1 = 156$

6. The correct answer is B.

Substitute 5 for the value of x to solve.

$x^2 + xy - y = 41$

$5^2 + 5y - y = 41$

25 + 5y − y = 41

25 − 25 + 5y − y = 41 − 25

5y − y = 16

4y = 16

4y ÷ 4 = 16 ÷ 4

y = 4

7. The correct answer is D.

In order to solve inequalities, deal with the whole numbers on each side of the equation first.

$$20 - \frac{3x}{4} \geq 17$$

$$(20 - 20) - \frac{3x}{4} \geq 17 - 20$$

$$-\frac{3x}{4} \geq -3$$

Then deal with the fraction.

$$-\frac{3x}{4} \geq -3$$

$$\left(4 \times -\frac{3x}{4}\right) \geq -3 \times 4$$

−3x ≥ −12

Then deal with the remaining whole numbers.

−3x ≥ −12

−3x ÷ 3 ≥ −12 ÷ 3

−x ≥ −4

Then deal with the negative number.

−x ≥ −4

−x + 4 ≥ −4 + 4

−x + 4 ≥ 0

Finally, isolate the unknown variable as a positive number.

−x + 4 ≥ 0

−x + x + 4 ≥ 0 + x

4 ≥ x

x ≤ 4

8. The correct answer is A.

First, you have to find the greatest common factor.

The factors of 18 are:

1 × 18 = 18

2 × 9 = 18

$3 \times 6 = 18$

The factors of 2 are:

$1 \times \mathbf{2} = 2$

So, put the integer for the common factor on the outside of the parentheses.

$18x^2 - 2x = 2(\quad)$

Then put the correct values into the parentheses.

$18x^2 - 2x = 2(9x^2 - x)$

Now determine whether there are any common variables for the terms that remain in the parentheses.

So, for $(9x^2 - x)$ we can see that $9x^2$ and x have the variable x in common.

Now factor out x to solve.

$2(9x^2 - x) =$

$2x(9x - 1)$

9. The correct answer is D.

Remember to perform the operations on the parentheses first and to be careful with negatives.

$(5x^2 + 3x - 4) - (6x^2 - 5x + 8) =$

$5x^2 + 3x - 4 - 6x^2 + 5x - 8$

Then place the terms containing x and y together.

$5x^2 + 3x - 4 - 6x^2 + 5x - 8 =$

$5x^2 - 6x^2 + 3x + 5x - 4 - 8$

Finally add or subtract the terms.

$5x^2 - 6x^2 + 3x + 5x - 4 - 8 =$

$-x^2 + 8x - 12$

10. The correct answer is A.

This is another application of the FOIL method.

FIRST: $(\mathbf{x} - 4)(\mathbf{3x} + 2)$

$x \times 3x = 3x^2$

OUTSIDE: $(\mathbf{x} - 4)(3x + \mathbf{2})$

$x \times 2 = 2x$

INSIDE: $(x - \mathbf{4})(\mathbf{3x} + 2)$

$-4 \times 3x = -12x$

LAST: $(x - \mathbf{4})(3x + \mathbf{2})$

$-4 \times 2 = -8$

Then add all of the above once you have completed FOIL.

$3x^2 + 2x + -12x + -8 =$

$3x^2 + 2x - 12x - 8 =$

$3x^2 - 10x - 8$

11. The correct answer is D.

This is a reverse FOIL type of problem. For any problem like this, the answer will be in the following format: $(x + ?)(x - ?)$. We know that the terms in the parentheses have to be in that format because we can get a negative number, like –20 above, only if we multiply a negative number and a positive number.

Next, we will look at the factors of 20:

$1 \times 20 = 20$

$2 \times 10 = 20$

$4 \times 5 = 20$

So, we know that we need to have a plus sign in one set of parentheses and a minus sign in the other set of parentheses because 20 is negative.

We also know that the factors of 20 need to be one number different than each other because the middle term is x, in other words $1x$.

The only factors of twenty that meet this criterion are 4 and 5.

Therefore the answer is $(x + 5)(x - 4)$.

12. The correct answer is C.

$(x - 4y)^2 = (x - 4y)(x - 4y)$

FIRST: $(\boldsymbol{x} - 4y)(\boldsymbol{x} - 4y)$

$x \times x = x^2$

OUTSIDE: $(\boldsymbol{x} - 4y)(x - \boldsymbol{4y})$

$x \times -4y = -4xy$

INSIDE: $(x - \boldsymbol{4y})(\boldsymbol{x} - 4y)$

$-4y \times x = -4xy$

LAST: $(x - \boldsymbol{4y})(x - \boldsymbol{4y})$

$-4y \times -4y = 16y^2$

SOLUTION:

$x^2 - 8xy + 16y^2$

13. The correct answer is B.

Do multiplication on the items in parentheses first.

$4x - 3(x + 2) = -3$

$4x - 3x - 6 = -3$

Then deal with the integers.

$4x - 3x - 6 = -3$

$4x - 3x - 6 + 6 = -3 + 6$

$4x - 3x = 3$

Then solve for x.

$4x - 3x = 3$

$x = 3$

14. The correct answer is A.

In order to solve the problem, you have to do division of the polynomial.

$$\begin{array}{r} x + 3 \\ x - 4{\overline{)x^2 - x - 12}} \\ \underline{x^2 - 4x} \\ 3x - 12 \\ \underline{3x - 12} \\ 0 \end{array}$$

15. The correct answer is A.

Multiply the numbers inside the square root signs first.

$6 \times 5 = 30$

Then put this result inside a square root symbol for your answer.

$\sqrt{30}$

16. The correct answer is D.

The area of a circle is always π times the radius squared.

Therefore, the area of circle A is: $3^2\pi = 9\pi$

Since the circles are internally tangent, the radius of circle B is calculated by taking the radius of circle A times 2.

In other words, the diameter of circle A is the radius of circle B.

Therefore, the radius of circle B is $3 \times 2 = 6$ and the area of circle B is $6^2\pi = 36\pi$.

To calculate the remaining area of circle B, we subtract as follows:

$36\pi - 9\pi = 27\pi$

17. The correct answer is C.

Perimeter is the measurement along the outside edge of a geometrical figure. Since the figure in this problem is a square, we know that the four sides are equal in length. To find the length of one side, we therefore divide the perimeter by four.

$24 \div 4 = 6$

Now we use the Pythagorean theorem to find the length of line segment AB.

Remember that the Pythagorean theorem states that the length of the hypotenuse is equal to the square root of the sum of the squares of the two other sides.

The hypotenuse is the part of a triangle that is opposite to the right angle, so in this case AB is the hypotenuse.

The hypotenuse length is the square root of $6^2 + 6^2$.

$\sqrt{6^2 + 6^2} =$

$\sqrt{36 + 36} = \sqrt{72}$

So, the answer is $\sqrt{72}$.

18. The correct answer is C.

The circumference of a circle is always calculated by using this formula:

Circumference = π × diameter

The diameter of a circle is always equal to the radius times 2.

So, the diameter for this circle is $4 \times 2 = 8$

Therefore, the circumference is 8π.

19. The correct answer is D.

Area of a circle = $\pi \times$ radius^2

The radius of this circle is 6.

$6^2 = 36$

Therefore, the area is 36π.

20. The correct answer is B.

We have the coordinates: (2, 2) and (4, –6).

Use the midpoint formula.

For two points on a graph (x_1, y_1) and (x_2, y_2), the midpoint is:

$(x_1 + x_2) \div 2$, $(y_1 + y_2) \div 2$

$(2 + 4) \div 2 =$ midpoint x, $(2 – 6) \div 2 =$ midpoint y

$6 \div 2 =$ midpoint x, $–4 \div 2 =$ midpoint y

$3 =$ midpoint x, $–2 =$ midpoint y

21. The correct answer is D.

The rectangular box has a base that is 5 inches wide and 6 inches long. The volume of a box is calculated by taking the length times the width times the height.

$5 \times 6 \times 10 = 300$

22. The correct answer is D.

The length of the hypotenuse is always the square root of the sum of the squares of the other two sides of the triangle.

hypotenuse length L = $\sqrt{M^2 + N^2}$

Now put in the values for the above problem.

L = $\sqrt{M^2 + N^2}$

L = $\sqrt{3^2 + 2^2}$

L = $\sqrt{9 + 4}$

L = $\sqrt{13}$

23. The correct answer is B.

This question is asking you to determine the value missing from a sample space when calculating probability. This is like other problems on probability, but we need to work backwards to find the missing value.

First, set up an equation to find the total items in the sample space. Then subtract the quantities of the known subsets from the total in order to determine the missing value.

We will use variable T as the total number of items in the set. The probability of getting a red scarf is $^1/_3$.

So, set up an equation to find the total items in the sample space.

We know that we have 5 red scarves, so put that in the numerator.

$\dfrac{5}{T} = \dfrac{1}{3}$

$$\frac{5}{T} \times 3 = \frac{1}{3} \times 3$$

$$\frac{5}{T} \times 3 = 1$$

$$\frac{15}{T} = 1$$

$$\frac{15}{T} \times T = 1 \times T$$

$$15 = T$$

So, we have 15 scarves in total. We have 5 red scarves, 6 blue scarves, and x green scarves in the total sample space, so now subtract the amount of red and blue scarves from the total in order to determine the number of green scarves.

$$5 + 6 + x = 15$$

$$11 + x = 15$$

$$11 - 11 + x = 15 - 11$$

$$x = 4$$

24. The correct answer is B.

Two angles are supplementary if they add up to 180 degrees.

25. The correct answer is A.

First, we need to find the circumference of the semicircle on the left side of the figure. The width of the rectangle of 10 inches forms the diameter of the semicircle, so the circumference of an entire circle with a diameter of 10 inches would be 10π inches.

We need the circumference for a semicircle only, which is half of a circle, so we need to divide the circumference by 2: $10\pi \div 2 = 5\pi$.

Since the right side of the figure is an equilateral triangle, the two sides of the triangle have the same length as the width of the rectangle, so all three sides are 10 inches each.

Finally, you need to add up the lengths of all of the sides to get the answer:

18 + 18 + 10 + 10 + 5π = 56 + 5π inches

1. Simplify: $(x - 2y)(2x - y)$
   A. $2x^2 - 3xy + 2y^2$
   B. $2x^2 + 3xy + 2y^2$
   C. $2x^2 - 5xy + 2y^2$
   D. $2x^2 - 5xy - 2y^2$

2. $20 + \dfrac{x}{4} \geq 22$, then $x \geq$?
   A. -8
   B. -2
   C. 0
   D. 8

3. State the x and y intercepts that fall on the straight line represented by the following equation:
   $y = x + 6$
   A. $(-6,0)$ and $(0,6)$
   B. $(0,6)$ and $(0,-6)$
   C. $(6,0)$ and $(0,-6)$
   D. $(0,-6)$ and $(6,0)$

4. $(5x + 7y) + (3x - 9y) = ?$
   A. $2x - 2y$
   B. $2x + 16y$
   C. $8x + 2y$
   D. $8x - 2y$

5. If $5x - 4(x + 2) = -2$, then $x = ?$
   A. 0
   B. 8
   C. 6
   D. -8

6). What is the cube root of 8?
   A. 64
   B. 4
   C. 3
   D. 2

7. Factor the following: $2xy - 8x^2y + 6y^2x^2$
   A. $2(xy - 4x^2y + 3x^2y^2)$
   B. $2xy(-4x + 3xy)$
   C. $2xy(1 - 4x + 3xy)$
   D. $2xy(1 + 4x - 3xy)$

8. If $x - 1 > 0$ and $y = x - 1$, then $y > ?$
    A. x
    B. $x + 1$
    C. $x - 1$
    D. 0

9. Find the coordinates (x, y) of the midpoint of the line segment on a graph that connects the points $(-5, 3)$ and $(3, -5)$.
    A. $(-1, -1)$
    B. $(-1, 1)$
    C. $(1, -1)$
    D. $(1, 1)$

10. Consider a two-dimensional linear graph where $x = 3$ and $y = 14$. The line crosses the y axis at 5. What is the slope of this line?
    A. 2.2
    B. 3.0
    C. 6.33
    D. −2.2

11. Factor the following equation: $6xy - 12x^2y - 24y^2x^2$
    A. $6(xy - 2x^2y - 4x^2y^2)$
    B. $xy(6 - 12x - 24xy)$
    C. $6xy(-2x - 4xy)$
    D. $6xy(1 - 2x - 4xy)$

12. If $x - 5 < 0$ and $y < x + 10$, then $y < ?$
    A. 5
    B. −5
    C. 0
    D. 15

13. Find the x and y intercepts of the following equation: $4x^2 + 9y^2 = 36$
    A. $(3,0)$ and $(0,2)$
    B. $(0,2)$ and $(0,3)$
    C. $(2,0)$ and $(3,0)$
    D. $(2,0)$ and $(0,3)$

14. If circle A has a radius of 0.4 and circle B has a radius of 0.2, what is the difference in area between the two circles?
    A. 0.04π
    B. 0.12π
    C. 0.16π
    D. 0.40π

15. $\sqrt{32} + 2\sqrt{72} + 3\sqrt{18} = ?$

 A. $2\sqrt{16} + 2\sqrt{36} + 3\sqrt{9}$

 B. $5\sqrt{122}$

 C. $25\sqrt{2}$

 D. $6\sqrt{122}$

16. $(-3x^2 + 7x + 2) - (x^2 - 5) = ?$
 A. $-2x^2 + 7x - 3$
 B. $-2x^2 + 7x + 7$
 C. $-4x^2 + 7x - 3$
 D. $-4x^2 + 7x + 7$

17. $\dfrac{5z-5}{z} \div \dfrac{6z-6}{5z^2} = ?$

 A. $\dfrac{6}{25z}$

 B. $\dfrac{30z^2 + 30}{5z^3}$

 C. $\dfrac{6z^2 - 6z}{25z^2 - 25z}$

 D. $\dfrac{25z}{6}$

18. If $c = \dfrac{a}{1-b}$, then $b = ?$

 A. $\dfrac{c}{a}$

 B. $\dfrac{a}{c} - 1$

 C. $-\dfrac{a}{c} + 1$

 D. $c - ca$

19. $8ab^2(3ab^4 + 2b) = ?$

    A. $11a^2b^6 + 10ab^3$

    B. $24a^2b^8 + 16ab^3$

    C. $48ab^6 + 32ab^2$

    D. $24a^2b^6 + 16ab^3$

20. Perform the operation and express as one fraction: $\dfrac{5}{12x} + \dfrac{4}{10x^2} = ?$

    A. $\dfrac{9}{22x^3}$

    B. $\dfrac{25x + 24}{60x^2}$

    C. $\dfrac{29}{12x}$

    D. $\dfrac{48x}{50x^2}$

21. The graph of $y = 8 \div (x - 4)$ is shown below.

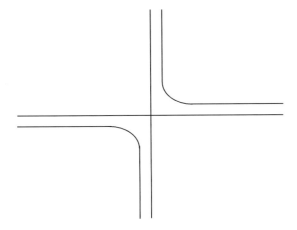

Which of the following is the best representation of $8 \div |\,(x - 4)\,|$?

A.

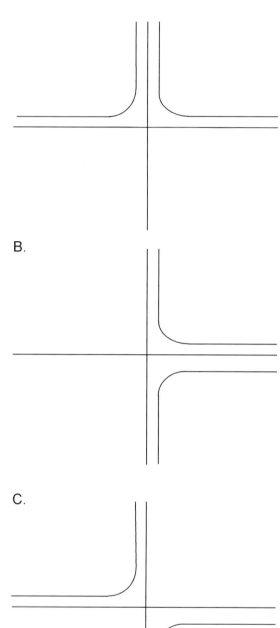

B.

C.

D.

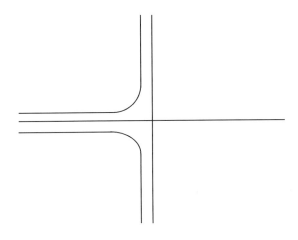

22. Which of the following is the graph of the solution set of −3x > 6?

A.

B.

C.

D.

23. In the figure below, *x* and *y* are parallel lines, and line *z* is a transversal crossing both *x* and *y*. Which three angles are equal in measure?

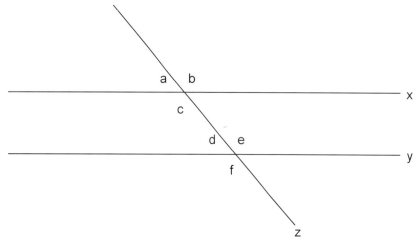

A. ∠a, ∠b, ∠c
B. ∠a, ∠c, ∠e
C. ∠b, ∠e, ∠f
D. ∠a, ∠d, ∠e

24. Becky rolls a fair pair of six-sided dice. One of the die is black and the other is red. Each die has values from 1 to 6. What is the probability that Becky will roll a 4 on the red die and a 5 on the black die?

A. $^1/_{36}$

B. $^2/_{36}$

C. $^1/_{12}$

D. $^2/_{12}$

25. The diagram below depicts a cell phone tower. The height of the tower from point B at the center of its base to point T at the top is 30 meters, and the distance from point B of the tower to point A on the ground is 18 meters. What is the approximate distance from point A on the ground to the top (T) of the cell phone tower?

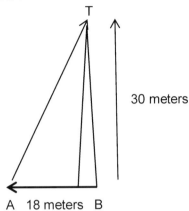

A 18 meters B

A. 10 meters
B. 20 meters
C. 30 meters
D. 35 meters

Practice Test 3 – Answers

1. C

2. D

3. A

4. D

5. C

6. D

7. C

8. D

9. A

10. B

11. D

12. D

13. A

14. B

15. C

16. D

17. D

18. C

19. D

20. B

21. A

22. B

23. C

24. A

25. D

Practice Test 3 – Explanations for the Answers

1. The correct answer is C.

Do not the word "simplify" confuse you. Just apply the FOIL method.

FIRST: $(\boldsymbol{x} - 2y)(\boldsymbol{2x} - y)$

$x \times 2x = 2x^2$

OUTSIDE: $(\boldsymbol{x} - 2y)(2x - \boldsymbol{y})$

$x \times -y = -xy$

INSIDE: $(x - \boldsymbol{2y})(\boldsymbol{2x} - y)$

$-2y \times 2x = -4xy$

LAST: $(x - \boldsymbol{2y})(2x - \boldsymbol{y})$

$-2y \times -y = 2y^2$

SOLUTION:

$2x^2 + -xy + -4xy + 2y^2 =$

$2x^2 - xy - 4xy + 2y^2 =$

$2x^2 - 5xy + 2y^2$

2. The correct answer is D.

Deal with the whole numbers first.

$20 + \dfrac{x}{4} \geq 22$

$20 - 20 + \dfrac{x}{4} \geq 22 - 20$

$\dfrac{x}{4} \geq 2$

Then eliminate the fraction.

$\dfrac{x}{4} \geq 2$

$4 \times \dfrac{x}{4} \geq 2 \times 4$

$x \geq 8$

3. The correct answer is A.

Remember that the y intercept exists where the line crosses the y axis, so $x = 0$ for the y intercept.

Begin by substituting 0 for x.

$y = x + 6$

$y = 0 + 6$

$y = 6$

Therefore, the coordinates (0, 6) represent the y intercept.

On the other hand, the x intercept exists where the line crosses the x axis, so $y = 0$ for the x intercept.

Now substitute 0 for y.

$y = x + 6$

$0 = x + 6$

$0 - 6 = x + 6 - 6$

$-6 = x$

So, the coordinates $(-6, 0)$ represent the x intercept.

4. The correct answer is D.

First perform the operations on the parentheses.

$(5x + 7y) + (3x - 9y) =$

$5x + 7y + 3x - 9y$

Then place the x and y terms together.

$5x + 7y + 3x - 9y =$

$5x + 3x + 7y - 9y$

Finally add and subtract to simplify.

$5x + 3x + 7y - 9y =$

$8x - 2y$

5. The correct answer is C.

Isolate the x variable in order to solve the problem.

$5x - 4(x + 2) = -2$

$5x - 4x - 8 = -2$

$x - 8 = -2$

$x - 8 + 8 = -2 + 8$

$x = 6$

6. The correct answer is D.

$2 \times 2 \times 2 = 8$

7. The correct answer is C.

First, figure out what variables are common to each term of the equation.

Let's look at the equation again.

$2xy - 8x^2y + 6y^2x^2$

We can see that each term contains x. We can also see that each term contains y.

So, now let's factor out xy.

$2xy - 8x^2y + 6y^2x^2 =$

$xy(2 - 8x + 6xy)$

Then, think about integers. We can see that all of the terms inside the parentheses are divisible by 2.

Now let's factor out the 2. In order to do this, we divide each term inside the parentheses by 2.

$xy(2 - 8x + 6xy) =$

$2xy(1 - 4x + 3xy)$

8. The correct answer is D.

Notice that both equations contain $x - 1$. Since the second equation has the equal sign, we can substitute y for $x - 1$ in the first equation.

$x - 1 > 0$

$x - 1 = y$

$y > 0$

9. The correct answer is A.

Remember that in order to find midpoints on a line, you need to use the midpoint formula.

For two points on a graph (x_1, y_1) and (x_2, y_2), the midpoint is:

$(x_1 + x_2) \div 2$, $(y_1 + y_2) \div 2$

$(-5 + 3) \div 2 = $ midpoint x, $(3 + -5) \div 2 = $ midpoint y

$-2 \div 2 = $ midpoint x, $-2 \div 2 = $ midpoint y

$-1 = $ midpoint x, $-1 = $ midpoint y

10. The correct answer is B.

When you are provided with a set of coordinates and the y intercept, you need the slope-intercept formula in order to calculate the slope of a line.

$y = mx + b$

In the slope-intercept formula, m is the slope and b is the y intercept, which is the point where the line crosses the y axis.

Here we have a two-dimensional linear graph where $x = 3$ and $y = 14$. The line crosses the y axis at 5.

Now solve for the numbers given in the problem.

$y = mx + b$

$14 = m3 + 5$

$14 - 5 = m3 + 5 - 5$

$9 = m3$

$9 \div 3 = m$

$3 = m$

11. The correct answer is D.

Find the variables are common to each term of the equation. We can see that each term contains x. We can also see that each term contains y.

So, now let's factor out xy.

$6xy - 12x^2y - 24y^2x^2 = $

$xy(6 - 12x - 24xy)$

Then, think about integers. We can see that all of the terms inside the parentheses are divisible by 6.

So, factor out the 6 by dividing each term inside the parentheses by 6.

$xy(6 - 12x - 24xy) = $

$6xy(1 - 2x - 4xy)$

12. The correct answer is D.

First solve the equation for x.

$x - 5 < 0$

$x - 5 + 5 < 0 + 5$

$x < 5$

Then solve for y by replacing x with its value.

$y < x + 10$

$y < 5 + 10$

$y < 15$

13. The correct answer is A.

Remember that for questions about x and y intercepts, you need to substitute 0 for x and then substitute 0 for y in order to solve the problem.

Here is the solution for y intercept:

$4x^2 + 9y^2 = 36$

$4(0x^2) + 9y^2 = 36$

$0 + 9y^2 = 36$

$9y^2 \div 9 = 36 \div 9$

$y^2 = 4$

$y = 2$

So, the y intercept is (0, 2)

Here is the solution for x intercept:

$4x^2 + 9y^2 = 36$

$4x^2 + 9(0y^2) = 36$

$4x^2 + 0 = 36$

$4x^2 \div 4 = 36 \div 4$

$x^2 = 9$

$x = 3$

So the x intercept is (3, 0)

14. The correct answer is B.

The area of circle A is $0.4^2\pi = 0.16\pi$

The area of circle B is $0.2^2\pi = 0.04\pi$

Then subtract: $0.16\pi - 0.04\pi = 0.12\pi$

15. The correct answer is C.

First you need to find the squared factors of the amounts inside the radical signs.

In this problem, 16, 36, and 9 are squared factors of each radical because $16 = 4^2$, $36 = 6^2$, and $9 = 3^2$.

$$\sqrt{32} + 2\sqrt{72} + 3\sqrt{18} =$$

$$\sqrt{2 \times 16} + 2\sqrt{2 \times 36} + 3\sqrt{2 \times 9}$$

Then expand the amounts inside the radicals for the factors and simplify.

$$\sqrt{2 \times 16} + 2\sqrt{2 \times 36} + 3\sqrt{2 \times 9} =$$

$$\sqrt{2 \times (4 \times 4)} + 2\sqrt{2 \times (6 \times 6)} + 3\sqrt{2 \times (3 \times 3)} =$$

$$4\sqrt{2} + (2 \times 6)\sqrt{2} + (3 \times 3)\sqrt{2} =$$

$4\sqrt{2} + 12\sqrt{2} + 9\sqrt{2} =$

$25\sqrt{2}$

16. The correct answer is D.

Remove the negative sign in front of the second set of parentheses by performing the operations on the double negative.

$(-3x^2 + 7x + 2) - (x^2 - 5) =$

$(-3x^2 + 7x + 2) - x^2 + 5$

Then remove the first set of parentheses.

$(-3x^2 + 7x + 2) - x^2 + 5 =$

$-3x^2 + 7x + 2 - x^2 + 5$

Then group like terms together to solve the problem.

$-3x^2 + 7x + 2 - x^2 + 5 =$

$-3x^2 - x^2 + 7x + 2 + 5 =$

$-4x^2 + 7x + 7$

17. The correct answer is D.

When dividing fractions, you need to invert the second fraction and then multiply the two fractions together.

$$\frac{5z - 5}{z} \div \frac{6z - 6}{5z^2} =$$

$$\frac{5z - 5}{z} \times \frac{5z^2}{6z - 6}$$

When multiplying fractions, you multiply the numerator of the first fraction by the numerator of the second fraction and then multiply the denominator of the first fraction by the denominator of the second fraction.

$$\frac{5z - 5}{z} \times \frac{5z^2}{6z - 6} =$$

$$\frac{5z^2(5z - 5)}{z(6z - 6)} =$$

$$\frac{25z^3 - 25z^2}{6z^2 - 6z}$$

Then look at the numerator and denominator from the result of the previous step to see if you can factor and simplify.

In this case, the numerator and denominator have the common factor of $(z^2 - z)$.

$$\frac{25z^3 - 25z^2}{6z^2 - 6z} =$$

$$\frac{25z(z^2 - z)}{6(z^2 - z)} =$$

$$\frac{25z}{6}$$

18. The correct answer is C.

First you need to get rid of the fraction. To eliminate the fraction, multiply each side of the equation by the denominator of the fraction.

$$c = \frac{a}{1-b}$$

$$c \times (1-b) = \frac{a}{1-b} \times (1-b)$$

$$c \times (1-b) = a$$

Then simplify the side of the equation with the variable that you need to isolate, in this case b.

$$c \times (1-b) = a$$

$$c(1-b) \div c = a \div c$$

$$1-b = \frac{a}{c}$$

Then isolate b by dealing with the integer and the negative sign in order to solve the problem.

$$1-b = \frac{a}{c}$$

$$1-1-b = \frac{a}{c} - 1$$

$$-b = \frac{a}{c} - 1$$

$$-b \times -1 = \left(\frac{a}{c} - 1\right) \times -1$$

$$b = -\frac{a}{c} + 1$$

19. The correct answer is D.

Remember to multiply the integers, but to add the exponents. Also remember that any variable times itself is equal to that variable squared. For example, $a \times a = a^2$

$$8ab^2(3ab^4 + 2b) =$$

$$(8ab^2 \times 3ab^4) + (8ab^2 \times 2b) =$$

$$24a^2b^6 + 16ab^3$$

20. The correct answer is B.

First you have to find the lowest common denominator (LCD).

For denominators that have integers and variables, you need two steps in order to find the LCD.

(1) Deal with the integers in the denominator.

(2) Then deal with the variable.

Our problem was: $\dfrac{5}{12x} + \dfrac{4}{10x^2} = ?$

In order to find the LCD, look at the denominators. What is the smallest possible number that is divisible by both 12 and by 10? The answer is 60.

Alternatively, find the factors of 12 and 10, and then multiply by the factor that they do not have in common.

12 = 2 × 6 and 10 = 2 × 5, so multiply 12 by 5 and 10 by 6 to arrive at 60 for the integer part of the denominator.

Then deal with the variable. $x = x \times 1$ and $x^2 = x \times x$, so multiply $x^2 \times 1$ and $x \times x$, to get x^2 for the variable part of the denominator.

Then put together the product of the LCD for the integer and the product of the LCD for the variable.

60 for the integer

x^2 for the variable

So, the LCD is $60x^2$.

$$\dfrac{5}{12x} + \dfrac{4}{10x^2} =$$

$$\left(\dfrac{5}{12x} \times \dfrac{5x}{5x} \right) + \left(\dfrac{4}{10x^2} \times \dfrac{6}{6} \right) = =$$

$$\dfrac{25x}{60x^2} + \dfrac{24}{60x^2} =$$

$$\dfrac{25x + 24}{60x^2}$$

21. The correct answer is A.

We know from the original graph in the question that when x is a positive number, then y will also be positive. This is represented by the curve in the upper right-hand quadrant of the graph.

We also know from the original graph in the question that when x is negative, y will also be negative. This is represented by the curve in the lower left-hand quadrant of the graph.

Next we need to determine the absolute value, which we covered in our Arithmetic Reasoning Study Guide.

You will remember from our ASVAB Arithmetic Reasoning Practice Tests book that absolute value is always a positive number.

If we add the absolute value symbols to the problem, then | $(x - 4)$ | will always result in a positive value for y.

Therefore, even when x is negative, y will be positive.

So, the curve originally represented in the lower left-hand quadrant of the graph must be shift into the *upper* left-hand quadrant.

22. The correct answer is B.

Isolate the unknown variable in order to solve the problem.

$-3x > 6$

127

$-3x \div 3 > 6 \div 3$

$-x > 2$

In order to solve the problem, we have to multiply each side of the equation by −1.

When we multiply both sides of an inequality by a negative number, we have to reverse the greater than symbol to a less than symbol (or if there is a less than symbol, we reverse it to a greater than symbol).

$-x > 2$

$-x \times -1 < 2 \times -1$

$x < -2$

In other words, if the isolated variable is *negative* as in this problem, you need to *reverse* the greater than symbol in order to make it the less than symbol.

$-x > 2$

$x < -2$

This is represented by line B.

23. The correct answer is C.

In problems like this, remember that parallel angles will be equal.

So, for example, angles a and d are equal, and angles b and e are equal.

Also remember that adjacent angles will be equal when bisected by two parallel lines, as with lines x and y in this problem.

Angles b and c are adjacent, and angles e and f are also adjacent.

So, ∠b, ∠e, and ∠f are equal.

24. The correct answer is A.

This is an advanced problem on understanding probability models.

For these questions, you will usually have two items, like two dice or two coins.

Each item will have various outcomes, like heads or tails for the coin or the different numbers on the die.

To solve problems like this one, it is usually best to write out the possible outcomes in a list.

This will help you visualize the number of possible outcomes that make up the sample space.

Then circle or highlight the events from the list to get your answer.

In this case, we have two items, each of which has a variable outcome. There are 6 numbers on the black die and 6 numbers on the red die.

Using multiplication, we can see that there are 36 possible combinations: 6 × 6 = 36

To check your answer, you can list the possibilities of the various combinations:

(1,1)   (1,2)   (1,3)   (1,4)   (1,5)   (1,6)
(2,1)   (2,2)   (2,3)   (2,4)   (2,5)   (2,6)
(3,1)   (3,2)   (3,3)   (3,4)   (3,5)   (3,6)
(4,1)   (4,2)   (4,3)   (4,4)   (4,5)   (4,6)
(5,1)   (5,2)   (5,3)   **(5,4)**   (5,5)   (5,6)
(6,1)   (6,2)   (6,3)   (6,4)   (6,5)   (6,6)

If the number on the left in each set of parentheses represents the black die and the number on the right represents the red die, we can see that there is one chance that Becky will roll a 4 on the red die and a 5 on the black die.

The result is expressed as a fraction, with the event (chance of the desired outcome) in the numerator and the total sample space (total possible combinations) in the denominator.

So, the answer is $^1/_{36}$.

25. The correct answer is D.

We need to use the Pythagorean theorem to solve the problem.

The Pythagorean theorem deals with right triangles.

The theorem helps us to calculate the length of the hypotenuse, which is the side opposite the right angle.

The right angle is at the $90°$ corner of the triangle.

The hypotenuse is called side C in the formula for the Pythagorean theorem.

The theorem states that the length of the hypotenuse is equal to the square root of the sum of the squares of the lengths of the two other sides (A and B).

So, we use the following formula to calculate the length of the hypotenuse:

In our problem we know that one side of the triangle is 18 meters and the other side of the triangle is 30 meters, so we can put these values into the formula in order to solve the problem.

$$\sqrt{A^2 + B^2} = C$$

$$\sqrt{18^2 + 30^2} = C$$

$$\sqrt{324 + 900} = C$$

$$\sqrt{1224} = C$$

$35 \times 35 = 1225$

So, the square root of 1224 is approximately 35.

$35 \approx C$

1. $8^7 \times 8^3 = ?$
   A. 8^4
   B. 8^{10}
   C. 8^{21}
   D. 64^{10}

2. Solve by elimination.

   $x + 5y = 24$

   $8x + 2y = 40$
   A. (4, 4)
   B. (–4, 4)
   C. (40, 4)
   D. (4, 38)

3. Perform the operation: $(4x - 3)(5x^2 + 12x + 11) = ?$
   A. $20x^3 + 33x^2 + 80x - 33$
   B. $20x^3 + 33x^2 + 80x + 33$
   C. $20x^3 + 33x^2 + 8x - 33$
   D. $20x^3 + 33x^2 - 8x - 33$

4. What equation of a straight line represents the slope-intercept formula for the following data?

   Through (4, 5); $m = -\dfrac{3}{5}$ and $b = \dfrac{37}{5}$

   A. $y = -\dfrac{3}{5}x + 5$

   B. $y = -\dfrac{12}{5}x - 5$

   C. $y = -\dfrac{3}{5}x - \dfrac{37}{5}$

   D. $y = -\dfrac{3}{5}x + \dfrac{37}{5}$

5. For all $a \neq b$, $\dfrac{\dfrac{5a}{b}}{\dfrac{2a}{a-b}} = ?$

   A. $\dfrac{10a^2}{ab - b^2}$

B. $\dfrac{a-b}{2b}$

C. $\dfrac{5a-5}{2}$

D. $\dfrac{5a-5b}{2b}$

6. Perform the operation and express as one fraction: $\dfrac{1}{a+1}+\dfrac{1}{a}$

   A. $\dfrac{2}{2a+1}$

   B. $\dfrac{a+1}{a}$

   C. $\dfrac{2a+1}{a^2+a}$

   D. $\dfrac{a^2+a}{2a+1}$

7. $\left(2+\sqrt{6}\right)^2 = ?$

   A. 8

   B. $8+2\sqrt{6}$

   C. $8+4\sqrt{6}$

   D. $10+4\sqrt{6}$

8. $\sqrt[3]{5} \times \sqrt[3]{7} = ?$

   A. $\sqrt[3]{13}$

   B. $\sqrt[6]{13}$

   C. $\sqrt[9]{13}$

   D. $\sqrt[3]{35}$

9. What is the value of $\dfrac{x-3}{2-x}$ when $x = 1$?

   A. 2

   B. -2

   C. $-\,^1/_2$

   D. $-\,^1/_2$

10. How many solutions exist for the following equation: $x^2 + 8 = 0$
    A. 0
    B. 1
    C. 2
    D. 4

11. If $5 + 5(3\sqrt{x} + 4) - 55$, then $\sqrt{x}$ = ?
    A. −4
    B. −2
    C. 2
    D. 4

12. Which one of the following is a solution to the following ordered pairs of equations?
    $y = -2x - 1$
    $y = x - 4$
    A. (0, 1)
    B. (1, −3)
    C. (4, 0)
    D. (1, 3)

13. For all positive integers x and y, $x - 6 < 0$ and $y < x + 12$, then $y < ?$
    A. 6
    B. 12
    C. 18
    D. 24

14. Which of the following is the graph of the solution of $2 + y < -8$?

A.

B.

C.

D.

−16   0

15. Find the area of the right triangle whose base is 2 and height is 5.
   A.   5
   B.   10
   C.   15
   D.   20

16. Consider a right-angled triangle, where side A and side B form the right angle, and side C is the hypotenuse. If A = 5 and C = $\sqrt{34}$, what is the length of side B?
   A.   8
   B.   3
   C. 34
   D. $\sqrt{34}$

17. Find the volume of a cone which has a radius of 3 and a height of 4.
   A. 4π
   B. 12π
   C. $\frac{4\pi}{3}$
   D. $\frac{3\pi}{4}$

18. The central angle in the circle below measures 45° and is subtended by Arc A which is 4π centimeters in length. How many centimeters long is the radius of this circle?

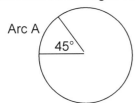

Arc A
45°

   A. 16
   B. 18
   C. 32
   D. $\pi \div 16$

19. In the figure below, XY and WZ are parallel, and lengths are provided in units. What is the area of trapezoid WXYZ in square units?

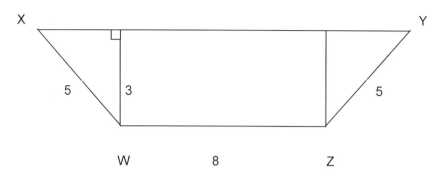

A. 24
B. 30
C. 34
D. 36

20. In the figure below, the lengths of KL, LM, and KN are provided in units. What is the area of triangle NLM in square units?

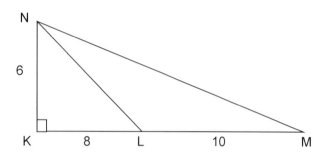

A. 24
B. 30
C. 48
D. 54

21. ∠XYZ is an isosceles triangle, where XY is equal to YZ. Angle Y is 30° and points W, X, and Z are co-linear. What is the measurement of ∠WXY?

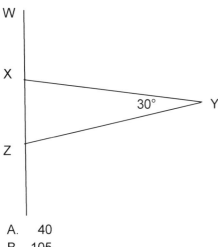

    A.   40
    B. 105
    C. 150
    D. 160

22. The triangle in the illustration below is an equilateral triangle. What is the measurement in degrees of angle a?

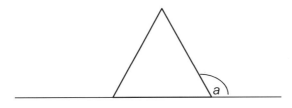

    A.   40
    B.   45
    C.   60
    D. 120

23. A box is manufactured to contain either laptop computers or notebook computers. When the computer systems are removed from the box, it is reused to hold other items. If the length of the box is 20cm, the width is 15cm, and the height is 25cm, what is the volume of the box?
    A. 1500
    B. 3000
    C. 7500
    D.   750

24. A football field is 100 yards long and 30 yards wide. What is the area of the football field in square yards?

    A.   130
    B.   150
    C.   300
    D. 3000
    E.

25. Which of the following statements about isosceles triangles is true?

    A.   Isosceles triangles have two equal sides.
    B.   When an altitude is drawn in an isosceles triangle, two equilateral triangles are formed.
    C.   The base of an isosceles triangle must be shorter than the length of each of the other two sides.
    D.   The sum of the measurements of the interior angles of an isosceles triangle must be equal to $360°$.

Practice Test 4 – Answers

1. B

2. A

3. C

4. D

5. D

6. C

7. D

8. D

9. B

10. A

11. C

12. B

13. C

14. B

15. A

16. B

17. B

18. A

19. D

20. B

21. B

22. D

23. C

24. D

25. A

Practice Test 4 – Explanations for the Answers

1. The correct answer is B.

This question tests your knowledge of exponent laws.

First look to see whether your base number is the same on each part of the equation.

In this question, 8 is the base number for each part of the equation.

If the base number is the same, and the problem asks you to multiply, you simply add the exponents.

$8^7 \times 8^3 =$

$8^{(7 + 3)} =$

8^{10}

If the base number is the same, and the problem asks you to *divide*, you *subtract* the exponents.

2. The correct answer is A.

We have the following equations:

$x + 5y = 24$

$8x + 2y = 40$

In order to solve by elimination, you need to subtract the second equation from the first equation.

Look at the term containing *x* in the second equation. We have 8*x* in the second equation.

In order to eliminate the term containing *x*, we need to multiply the first equation by 8.

$x + 5y = 24$

$(8 \times x) + (5y \times 8) = (24 \times 8)$

$8x + 40y = 192$

Now do the subtraction.

$$8x + 40y = 192$$
$$\underline{-(8x + 2y = 40)}$$
$$38y = 152$$

Then solve for y.

$38y = 152$

$38y \div 38 = 152 \div 38$

$y = 4$

Now put the value for *y* into the first equation and solve for *x*.

$x + 5y = 24$

$x + (5 \times 4) = 24$

$x + 20 = 24$

$x + 20 - 20 = 24 - 20$

$x = 4$

Therefore, $x = 4$ and $y = 4$, so the answer is (4, 4).

3. The correct answer is C.

For problems like this one, you need to multiply the first term in the first set of parentheses by all of the terms in the second set of parentheses.

Then multiply the second term in the first set of parentheses by all of the terms in the second set of parentheses.

So, you need to multiply as shown.

$$(4x - 3)(5x^2 + 12x + 11) =$$

$$[(4x \times 5x^2) + (4x \times 12x) + (4x \times 11)] - [(3 \times 5x^2) + (3 \times 12x) + (3 \times 11)] =$$

$$(20x^3 + 48x^2 + 44x) - (15x^2 + 36x + 33)$$

Then simplify, remembering to be careful about the negative sign in front of the second set of parentheses.

$$(20x^3 + 48x^2 + 44x) - (15x^2 + 36x + 33) =$$

$$(20x^3 + 48x^2 + 44x) - 15x^2 - 36x - 33 =$$

$$20x^3 + 48x^2 - 15x^2 + 44x - 36x - 33 =$$

$$20x^3 + 33x^2 + 8x - 33$$

4. The correct answer is D.

You will remember that the slope intercept formula is: $y = mx + b$

Remember that m is the slope and b is the y intercept.

From the question, we know that we have a line that passes through point (4, 5) with a slope of $m = -\dfrac{3}{5}$

We also know that $b = \dfrac{37}{5}$.

Now put the values for m and b into the slope intercept formula.

$y = mx + b$

$$y = -\frac{3}{5}x + \frac{37}{5}$$

5. The correct answer is D.

When you have fractions in the numerator and denominator of another fraction, you can divide the two fractions as shown.

$$\frac{\dfrac{5a}{b}}{\dfrac{2a}{a-b}} = \frac{5a}{b} \div \frac{2a}{a-b}$$

Then invert and multiply just like you would for any other fraction.

$$\frac{5a}{b} \div \frac{2a}{a-b} =$$

$$\frac{5a}{b} \times \frac{a-b}{2a} =$$

$$\frac{5a^2 - 5ab}{2ab}$$

Then simplify, if possible.

$$\frac{5a^2 - 5ab}{2ab} =$$

$$\frac{a(5a - 5b)}{a(2b)} =$$

$$\frac{5a - 5b}{2b}$$

6. The correct answer is C.

Find the lowest common denominator.

$$\frac{1}{a+1} + \frac{1}{a} =$$

$$\left(\frac{1}{a+1} \times \frac{a}{a} \right) + \left(\frac{1}{a} \times \frac{a+1}{a+1} \right) =$$

$$\frac{a}{a^2 + a} + \frac{a+1}{a^2 + a}$$

Then simplify, if possible.

$$\frac{a}{a^2 + a} + \frac{a+1}{a^2 + a} =$$

$$\frac{a + a + 1}{a^2 + a} =$$

$$\frac{2a + 1}{a^2 + a}$$

7. The correct answer is D.

Don't worry about the radical. Just perform the operations.

$$(2 + \sqrt{6})^2 =$$

$$(2 + \sqrt{6})(2 + \sqrt{6}) =$$

First . . . Outside . . Inside . . . Last

$$(2 \times 2) + (2 \times \sqrt{6}) + (2 \times \sqrt{6}) + (\sqrt{6} \times \sqrt{6}) =$$

$$(2 \times 2) + (2\sqrt{6} + 2\sqrt{6}) + \sqrt{6}^2 =$$

$4 + 4\sqrt{6} + 6 =$

$10 + 4\sqrt{6}$

8. The correct answer is D.

Remember for problems like this, you need to multiply the amounts inside the square root sign, but leave the cube root as it is.

$\sqrt[3]{5} \times \sqrt[3]{7} = \sqrt[3]{35}$

9. The correct answer is B.

We have the fraction $\dfrac{x-3}{2-x}$ and we know that x = 1.

Substitute 1 for x.

$\dfrac{x-3}{2-x} =$

$\dfrac{1-3}{2-1} =$

$(1 - 3) \div (2 - 1) =$

$-2 \div 1 =$

-2

10. The correct answer is A.

Remember that any real number squared will always equal a positive number.

Since 8 is added to the first value x^2, the result will always be 8 or greater.

In other words, since x^2 is always a positive number, the result of the equation would never be 0.

So, there are zero solutions for this equation.

11. The correct answer is C.

First, deal with the integers that are outside the parentheses.

$5 + 5(3\sqrt{x} + 4) = 55$

$5 + 15\sqrt{x} + 20 = 55$

$25 + 15\sqrt{x} = 55$

$25 - 25 + 15\sqrt{x} = 55 - 25$

$15\sqrt{x} = 30$

Then divide in order to isolate $\sqrt{x}$.

$15\sqrt{x} = 30$

$(15\sqrt{x}) \div 15 = 30 \div 15$

$\sqrt{x} = 2$

12. The correct answer is B.

141

We have the ordered pair of equations:

$y = -2x - 1$

$y = x - 4$

We have the answer choices:

A. (0, 1)

B. (1, −3)

C. (4, 0)

D. (1, 3)

So, plug in values for x and y from the answer choices to see if they work for both equations.

Answer choice (B) is the only answer that works for both equations.

If $x = 1$

then for $y = -2x - 1$

$y = (-2 \times 1) - 1$

$y = -2 - 1$

$y = -3$

For the second equation:

$y = x - 4$

$-3 = x - 4$

$-3 + 4 = x - 4 + 4$

$-3 + 4 = x$

$1 = x$

13. The correct answer is C.

Our question stated that for all positive integers x and y: $x - 6 < 0$ and $y < x + 12$.

To solve inequalities like this one, you should first solve the equation for x.

$x - 6 < 0$

$x - 6 + 6 < 0 + 6$

$x < 6$

Now solve for y by replacing x with its value.

$y < x + 12$

$y < 6 + 12$

$y < 18$

14. The correct answer is B.

Our problem asked for the solution of $2 + y < -8$

Isolate y in order to solve the problem.

$2 + y < -8$

$2 - 2 + y < -8 - 2$

$y < -10$

15. The correct answer is A.

We have a right triangle whose base is 2 and height is 5.

Use the formula for triangle area = (base × height) ÷ 2

Now substitute the amounts for base and height.

area = (5 × 2) ÷ 2 = 10 ÷ 2 = 5

16. The correct answer is B.

We have a right-angled triangle, where side A and side B form the right angle, and side C is the hypotenuse. A = 5 and C = $\sqrt{34}$, so use the Pythagorean theorem to solve for B.

hypotenuse length C = $\sqrt{A^2 + B^2}$

$\sqrt{34}$ = $\sqrt{25 + B^2}$

$B^2 = 9$

$B = 3$

17. The correct answer is B.

Our cone has a radius of 3 and a height of 4.

Cone volume = (π × radius^2 × height) ÷ 3

Substitute the values for base and height.

volume = (π3^2 × 4) ÷ 3 =

(π9 × 4) ÷ 3 =

π36 ÷ 3 = 12π

18. The correct answer is A.

Circumference = π × radius × 2

The angle given in the problem is 45°.

If we divide the total 360° in the circle by the 45° angle, we have: 360 ÷ 45 = 8

So, there are 8 such arcs along this circle.

We then have to multiply the number of arcs by the length of each arc to get the circumference of the circle.

8 × 4π = 32π (circumference)

Then, use the formula for the circumference of the circle to solve.

32π = π × 2 × radius

32π ÷ 2 = π × 2 × radius ÷ 2

16π = π × radius

16 = radius

19. The correct answer is D.

First, calculate the area of the central rectangle.

Remember that the area of a rectangle is length times height.

8 × 3 = 24

Using the Pythagorean theorem, we know that the base of each triangle is 4.

5 = $\sqrt{3^2 + base^2}$

5^2 = 3^2 + base^2

$25 = 9 + base^2$

$25 - 9 = 9 - 9 + base^2$

$16 = base^2$

$4 = base$

Then calculate the area of each of the triangles on each side of the central rectangle.

Remember that the area of a triangle is base times height divided by 2.

$(4 \times 3) \div 2 = 6$

So, the total area is the area of the main rectangle plus the area of each of the two triangles.

$24 + 6 + 6 = 36$

20. The correct answer is B.

Remember that the area of a triangle is base times height divided by 2

First, calculate the area of triangle NKM.

$[6 \times (8 + 10)] \div 2 =$

$(6 \times 18) \div 2 =$

$108 \div 2 = 54$

Then, calculate the area of the area of triangle NKL.

$(6 \times 8) \div 2 = 24$

The remaining triangle NLM is then calculated by subtracting the area of triangle NKL from triangle NKM.

$54 - 24 = 30$

21. The correct answer is B.

We know that any straight line is 180°.

We also know that the sum of the degrees of the three angles of any triangle is 180°.

The sum of angles X, Y, and Z = 180

So, the sum of angle X and angle Z equals $180° - 30° = 150°$.

Remember that in an isosceles triangle, the angles at the base of the triangle are equal.

Because this triangle is isosceles, angle X and angle Z are equivalent.

So, we can divide the remaining degrees by 2 as follows:

$150° \div 2 = 75°$

In other words, angle X and angle Z are each 75°.

Then we need to subtract the degree of the angle $\angle XYZ$ from 180° for the straight line to get the measurement of $\angle WXY$.

$180° - 75° = 105°$

22. The correct answer is D.

An equilateral triangle has three equal sides and three equal angles. Since all 3 angles in any triangle need to add up to 180 degrees, each angle of an equilateral triangle is 60 degrees ($180 \div 3 = 60$). Angles that lie along the same side of a straight line must add up to 180. So, we calculate angle a as follows:

$180 - 60 = 120$

23. The correct answer is C.

To calculate the volume of a box, you need the formula from above:

volume = base × width × height

Now substitute the values from the problem into the formula.

volume = 20 × 15 × 25

volume = 7500

24. The correct answer is D.

The area of a rectangle is equal to its length times its width.

This football field is 30 yards wide and 100 yards long, we now we can substitute the values.

rectangle area = width × length

rectangle area = 30 × 100

rectangle area = 3000

25. The correct answer is A.

An isosceles triangle has two equal sides, so answer A is correct.

If an altitude is drawn in an isosceles triangle, we have to put a straight line down the middle of the triangle from the peak to the base. Dividing the triangle in this way would form two right triangles, rather than two equilateral triangles. So, answer B is incorrect.

The base of an isosceles triangle can be longer than the length of each of the other two sides, so answer C is incorrect.

The sum of all three angles of any triangle must be 180 degrees, rather than 360 degrees. So, answer D is incorrect.

By definition a triangle must have three sides. Also remember that all three angles inside the triangle must add up to 180 degrees and that right angles measure 90 degrees.

Therefore, the angles opposite the two equal sides of an isosceles triangle cannot be right triangles because 2 × 90° = 180°. In this case, there would be no room for the third angle. So, answer E is incorrect.

1. What are two possible values of x for the following equation? $x^2 + 6x + 8 = 0$
   A. 1 and 2
   B. 2 and 4
   C. 6 and 8
   D. −2 and −4

2. If $\dfrac{30}{\sqrt{x^2 - 75}} = 6$, then $x = $?
   A. 100
   B. 30
   C. 25
   D. 10

3. $3^4 \times 3^3 = $?
   A. 3^7
   B. 9^7
   C. 6^{12}
   D. 9^{12}

4. Evaluate the expression $2(x + 2)(x - 3)$ if $x = 5$
   A. 6
   B. 12
   C. 28
   D. 32

5. A company sells jeans and T-shirts. J represents jeans and T represents T-shirts in the equations below.

   $2J + T = \$50$
   $J + 2T = \$40$

   Sarah buys one pair of jeans and one T-shirt. How much does she pay for her entire purchase?
   A. $10
   B. $30
   C. $20
   D. $70

6. Which of the answers below is equal to $\sqrt{45}$?
   A. $1 \div 45$
   B. $5\sqrt{9}$
   C. $9\sqrt{5}$
   D. $3\sqrt{5}$

7. The term PPM, pulses per minute, is used to determine how many heartbeats an individual has every 60 seconds. In order to calculate PPM, the pulse is taken for ten seconds, represented by variable P. What equation is used to calculate PPM?
    A. PPM ÷ 60
    B. PPM ÷ 10
    C. P6
    D. P10

8. A runner of a 100 mile endurance race ran at a speed of 5 miles per hour for the first 80 miles of the race and x miles per hour for the last 20 miles of the race. What equation represents the runner's average speed for the entire race?
    A. $100 \div [(80 \div 5) + (20 \div x)]$
    B. $100 \times [(80 \div 5) + (20 \div x)]$
    C. $100 \div [(80 \times 5) + (20 \times x)]$
    D. $100 \times [(80 \times 5) + (20 \times x)]$

9. The number of bottles of soda that a soft drink factory can produce during D number of days using production method A is represented by the following equation: $D^5 + 12,000$
    Alternatively, the number of bottles of soda that can be produced using production method B is represented by this equation: $D \times 10,000$
    What is the largest number of bottles of soda that can be produced by the factory during a 10 day period?
    A. 10,000
    B. 12,000
    C. 100,000
    D. 112,000

10. If $\frac{3}{4}x - 2 = 4$, $x = $?
    A. $\frac{8}{3}$
    B. $\frac{1}{8}$
    C. 8
    D. −8

11. Simplify: $(x + 5) - (x^2 - 2x)$
    A. $-x - x^2 + 5$
    B. $-x + x^2 - 5$
    C. $x - x^2 + 5$
    D. $3x - x^2 + 5$

12. What is the value of the expression $2x^2 + 3xy - y^2$ when $x = 3$ and $y = -3$?
    A. −18
    B. 0
    C. 18
    D. 36

13. What ordered pair is a solution to the following system of equations?

$x + y = 9$

$xy = 20$

    A. (2, 7)

    B. (2,10)

    C. (3, 6)

    D. (4, 5)

14. $5^8 \div 5^2 = ?$

    A. 25^6

    B. 25^4

    C. 5^6

    D. 5^4

15. What is the value of $(3x^2 + 2x - 3) - (4x - 2)$ when $x = -2$?

    A. −1

    B. 15

    C. 13

    D. −9

16. If $x + y = 5$ and $a + b = 4$, what is the value of $(3x + 3y)(5a + 5b)$?

    A.   9

    B.   35

    C. 200

    D. 300

17. Consider the inequality: $-3x + 14 < 5$

Which of the following values of x is a possible solution to the inequality above?

    A. −3.1

    B. 2.80

    C. 2.25

    D. 3.15

18. A small circle has a radius of 5 inches, and a larger circle has a radius of 8 inches. What is the difference in inches between the circumferences of the two circles?

    A. 3

    B. 6

    C. 6π

    D. 9π

19. Which of the following dimensions would be needed in order to find the area of the figure?

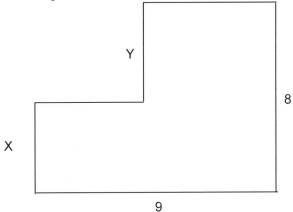

A. X only
B. Y only
C. Both X and Y
D. Neither X nor Y

20. The base (B) of the cylinder in the illustration shown below is at a right angle to its sides. The radius (R) of the base of cylinder measures 5 centimeters. The height (H) is 10 centimeters. What is the volume of this cylinder?

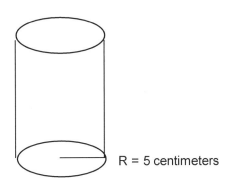

R = 5 centimeters

A. 250π
B. 100π
C. 50π
D. 500π

21. The illustration below shows a right circular cone which has a base radius of 4 and a height of 9.

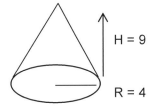

H = 9

R = 4

What is the volume of the cone?

A. 148π

B. 108π

C. 48π

D. 24π

22. A farmer has a rectangular pen in which he keeps animals. He has decided to divide the pen into two parts. To divide the pen, he will erect a fence diagonally from the two corners, as shown in the diagram below. How long in yards is the diagonal fence?

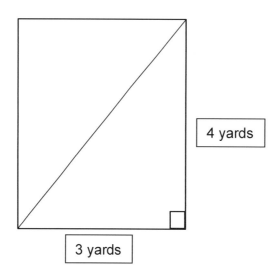

4 yards

3 yards

A. 5

B. 5.5

C. 6

D. 6.5

23. Consider this equation for a straight line: $3x - 4y + 3 = 0$
What is the y intercept?

A. 3

B. 4

C. $^3/_4$

D. $-\,^{3/4}$

24. The figure below shows a right triangular prism. Side AB measures 4 units, side AC measures 3.5 units, and side BD measures 5 units. What amount below best approximates the surface area of rectangle BCDE?

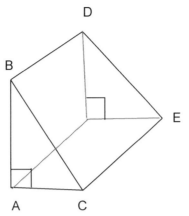

A. 66.5
B. 26.5
C. 74
D. 78.00

25. Which of the following statements about parallelograms is false?
   A. A parallelogram has no right angles.
   B. A parallelogram has opposite angles which are congruent.
   C. A parallelogram has two pairs of parallel sides.
   D. A rectangle is a parallelogram.

Practice Test 5 – Answers

1. D

2. D

3. A

4. C

5. B

6. D

7. C

8. A

9. D

10. C

11. D

12. A

13. D

14. C

15. B

16. D

17. D

18. C

19. C

20. A

21. C

22. B

23. C

24. B

25. A

Practice Test 5 – Explanations for the Answers

1. The correct answer is D.

STEP 1: Factor the equation.

$x^2 + 6x + 8 = 0$

$(x + 2)(x + 4) = 0$

STEP 2: Now substitute 0 for x in the first pair of parentheses.

$(0 + 2)(x + 4) = 0$

$2(x + 4) = 0$

$2x + 8 = 0$

$2x + 8 - 8 = 0 - 8$

$2x = -8$

$2x \div 2 = -8 \div 2$

$x = -4$

STEP 3: Then substitute 0 for x in the second pair of parentheses.

$(x + 2)(x + 4) = 0$

$(x + 2)(0 + 4) = 0$

$(x + 2)4 = 0$

$4x + 8 = 0$

$4x + 8 - 8 = 0 - 8$

$4x = -8$

$4x \div 4 = -8 \div 4$

$x = -2$

2. The correct answer is D.

Eliminate the radical in the denominator by multiplying both sides of the equation by the radical.

$$\frac{30}{\sqrt{x^2 - 75}} = 6$$

$$\frac{30}{\sqrt{x^2 - 75}} \times \sqrt{x^2 - 75} = 6 \times \sqrt{x^2 - 75}$$

$$30 = 6\sqrt{x^2 - 75}$$

Then eliminate the integer in front of the radical.

$$30 = 6\sqrt{x^2 - 75}$$

$$30 \div 6 = \left(6\sqrt{x^2 - 75}\right) \div 6$$

$$5 = \sqrt{x^2 - 75}$$

Then eliminate the radical by squaring both sides of the equation, and solve for x.

$$5 = \sqrt{x^2 - 75}$$

$$5^2 = \left(\sqrt{x^2 - 75}\right)^2$$

$$25 = x^2 - 75$$

$$25 + 75 = x^2 - 75 + 75$$

$$100 = x^2$$

$$x = 10$$

3. The correct answer is A.

Remember to add the exponents when multiplying.

$$3^4 \times 3^3 = 3^{3+4} = 3^7$$

4. The correct answer is C.

$2(x + 2)(x - 3)$ and $x = 5$

$2(5 + 2)(5 - 3) = 2 \times 7 \times 2 = 28$

5. The correct answer is B.

In order to solve the problem, take the second equation and isolate J on one side of the equation. By doing this, you define variable J in terms of variable T.

$J + 2T = \$40$

$J + 2T - 2T = \$40 - 2T$

$J = \$40 - 2T$

Now substitute $\$40 - 2T$ for variable J in the first equation to solve for variable T.

$2J + T = 50$

$2(40 - 2T) + T = 50$

$80 - 4T + T = 50$

$80 - 3T = 50$

$80 - 3T + 3T = 50 + 3T$

$80 = 50 + 3T$

$80 - 50 = 50 - 50 + 3T$

$30 = 3T$

$30 \div 3 = 3T \div 3$

$10 = T$

So, now that we know that a T-shirt costs $10, we can substitute this value in one of the equations in order to find the value for the jeans, which is variable J.

$2J + T = 50$

$2J + 10 = 50$

$2J + 10 - 10 = 50 - 10$

$2J = 40$

$2J \div 2 = 40 \div 2$

$J = 20$

Now solve for Sarah's purchase. If she purchased one pair of jeans and one T-shirt, then she paid:

$\$10 + \$20 = \$30$

6. The correct answer is D.

For square root problems like this one, you need to remember certain mathematical principles.

First, remember to factor the number inside the square root sign.

The factors of 45 are:

1 × 45 = 45

3 × 15 = 45

5 × 9 = 45

Then look to see if any of these factors have square roots that are whole numbers.

In this case, the only factor whose square root is a whole number is 9.

Now find the square root of 9.

$\sqrt{9} = 3$

Finally, you need to put this number at the front of the square root sign and put the other factor inside the square root sign in order to solve the problem.

$\sqrt{45} =$

$\sqrt{9 \times 5} =$

$\sqrt{3 \times 3 \times 5} =$

$3\sqrt{5}$

7. The correct answer is C.

Since there are 60 seconds in a minute, and pulse is measured in 10 second units, we divide the seconds as follows: 60 ÷ 10 = 6

Accordingly, the PPM is calculated by talking P times 6: PPM = P6

8. The correct answer is A.

Miles per hour (MPH) is calculated as follows:

miles ÷ hours = MPH

So, if we have the MPH and the miles traveled, we need to change the above equation in order to calculate the hours.

miles ÷ hours = MPH

miles ÷ hours × hours = MPH × hours

miles = MPH × hours

miles ÷ MPH = (MPH × hours) ÷ MPH

miles ÷ MPH = hours

In other words, we divide the number of miles by the miles per hour to get the time for each part of the race.

So, for the first part of the race, the hours are calculated as follows:

80 ÷ 5

For the second part of the race, we take the remaining mileage and divide by the unknown variable.

20 ÷ x

Since the race is divided into two parts, these two results added together equal the total time.

Total time = [(80 ÷ 5) + (20 ÷ x)]

The total amount of miles for the race is then divided by the total time to get the average miles per hour for the entire race.

That is because MPH is calculated as follows:

MPH = miles ÷ hours

We have a 100 mile race, so the result is:

100 ÷ [(80 ÷ 5) + (20 ÷ x)]

9. The correct answer is D.

First we have to calculate the output for our first production method. For 10 days:

D^5 + 12,000 =

10^5 + 12,000 =

100,000 + 12,000 =

112,000

Then we have to calculate the output for the other production method.

10 × 10,000 = 100,000

112,000 is greater than the 100,000 amount that method B yields.

So, the greatest amount of production for 10 days is 112,000 bottles.

10. The correct answer is C.

This is a problem requiring you to solve an expression that contains a single variable, a fraction, and integers. First, isolate the integers and then eliminate the fraction. Finally, divide to find the value of the variable.

Isolate the integers to one side of the equation.

$\frac{3}{4}x - 2 = 4$

$\frac{3}{4}x - 2 + 2 = 4 + 2$

$\frac{3}{4}x = 6$

Then get rid of the fraction by multiplying both sides by the denominator.

$\frac{3}{4}x \times 4 = 6 \times 4$

$3x = 24$

Then divide to solve the problem.

$3x \div 3 = 24 \div 3$

$x = 8$

11. The correct answer is D.

To simplify, remove the parentheses, paying attention to the negative sign in front of the second set of parentheses.

$(x + 5) - (x^2 - 2x) =$

$x + 5 - x^2 + 2x$

Now simplify for the common terms.

$x + 5 - x^2 + 2x =$

$x + 2x + 5 - x^2 =$

$x + 2x - x^2 + 5 =$

$3x - x^2 + 5$

12. The correct answer is A.

Here we have the expression $2x^2 + 3xy - y^2$ and we know that $x = 3$ and $y = -3$.

Put in the values for x and y and multiply.

$2x^2 + 3xy - y^2 =$

$(2 \times 3^2) + (3 \times 3 \times - 3) - (-3^2) =$

$(2 \times 3 \times 3) + (3 \times 3 \times - 3) - (-3 \times -3) =$

$(2 \times 9) + (3 \times -9) - (9) =$

$18 + (-27) - 9 =$

$18 - 27 - 9 =$

$18 - 36 =$

-18

13. The correct answer is D.

For questions on systems of equations like this one, you should look at the multiplication equation first.

Ask yourself, what are the factors of 20? We know that 20 is the product of the following:

$1 \times 20 = 20$

$2 \times 10 = 20$

$4 \times 5 = 20$

Now add each of the two factors together to solve the first equation.

$1 + 20 = 21$

$2 + 10 = 12$

$4 + 5 = 9$

(4, 5) solves both equations, so it is the correct answer.

14. The correct answer is C.

If the base number is the same, and the problem asks you to divide, you subtract the exponents.

$5^8 \div 5^2 = 5^{8-2} = 5^6$

15. The correct answer is B.

We have the equation $(3x^2 + 2x - 3) - (4x - 2)$ and we know that $x = -2$.

Remove the parentheses first.

$(3x^2 + 2x - 3) - (4x - 2) =$

$(3x^2 + 2x - 3) - 4x - (-2) =$

$3x^2 + 2x - 3 - 4x + 2$

Then substitute for x to solve.

$3x^2 + 2x - 3 - 4x + 2 =$

$(3 \times -2^2) + (2 \times -2) - 3 - (4 \times -2) + 2 =$

$12 - 4 - 3 + 8 + 2 = 15$

16. The correct answer is D.

This problem involves expressions that contain more than one variable. First of all, factor each parenthetical in the final expression. Then substitute values in order to solve the problem.

Factor each of the parentheticals in the expression provided in the problem:

$(3x + 3y)(5a + 5b) =$

$3(x + y) \times 5(a + b)$

We know that $x + y = 5$ and $a + b = 4$, so we can substitute the values stated for each of the parentheticals:

$3(x + y) \times 5(a + b) =$

$3(5) \times 5(4) =$

$15 \times 20 = 300$

17. The correct answer is D.

Place the integers on one side of the inequality.

$-3x + 14 < 5$

$-3x + 14 - 14 < 5 - 14$

$-3x < -9$

Then get rid of the negative number. We need to reverse the way that the inequality sign points because we are dividing.

$-3x < -9$

$-3x \div -3 > -9 \div -3$ ("Less than" becomes "greater than" because we divide by a negative number.)

$x > 3$

3.15 is greater than 3, so it is the correct answer.

18. The correct answer is C.

Use the formula: (2 × π × radius)

So, we calculate the circumference of the large circle as: 2 × π × 8 = 16π

The circumference of the small circle is: 2 × π × 5 = 10π

Then, we subtract to get our solution: 16π – 10π = 6π

19. The correct answer is C.

This question is asking you to calculate the area of a hybrid shape. To solve problems like this one, try to visualize two rectangles. The first rectangle would measure 8 × 9 and the second rectangle would measure X × Y.

Essentially a rectangle is missing at the upper left-hand corner of the figure.

We would need to know both the length and width of the "missing" rectangle in order to calculate the area of our figure.

So, we need to know both X and Y in order to solve the problem.

20. The correct answer is A.

The formula to calculate the volume of a cylinder is as follows:

Volume of cylinder = $\pi R^2 h = \pi \times radius^2 \times height$

Our radius is 5 and our height in 10 in this problem.

$\pi \times 5^2 \times 10 = = \pi \times 25 \times 10 = 250\pi$

21. The correct answer is C.

The formula for the volume of a cone is:

$$\frac{\pi R^2 H}{3}$$

(π × radius squared × height) ÷ 3

Substitute the values to solve.

(π × 4^2 × 9) ÷ 3 = 48π

22. The correct answer is B.

The two sides of the field form a right angle, so we can use the Pythagorean theorem to solve the problem: $\sqrt{3^2 + 4^2} = \sqrt{9 + 16} = \sqrt{25} = 5$

23. The correct answer is C.

To find the point at which the line intersects the y axis, substitute 0 for x.

$3x - 4y + 3 = 0$

$0x - 4y + 3 = 0$

$-4y + 3 = 0$

$-4y + 3 - 3 = 0 - 3$

$-4y = -3$

$y = {}^3/_4$

24. The correct answer is B.

You will need the Pythagorean theorem for this problem, as well as the formula for the area of a rectangle.

Area of a rectangle = L × W = Length × Width

Area of a triangle = bH ÷ 2 = base × height ÷ 2

First of all, we need to find the length of the hypotenuse (side BC).

Since AB is 4 units and AC is 3.5 units, we can use the Pythagorean theorem as follows:

$\sqrt{3.5^2 + 4^2} = \sqrt{12.25 + 16} = \sqrt{28.25} \approx 5.3$

We know that side BD measures 5 units, so we can then calculate the surface area of the sloping rectangle that lies along the hypotenuse (side ABCD) as:

Length × Width = 5.3 × 5 = 26.5

25. The correct answer is A.

The opposite or facing sides of a parallelogram are of equal length and the opposite angles of a parallelogram are of equal measure. You will recall that congruent is another word for equal in measure. So, answer B is true.

A parallelogram is a four-sided figure that has two pairs of parallel sides, so answer C is true.

A rectangle is a parallelogram with four right angles, so answer D is true, but answer A is false.

Made in the USA
San Bernardino, CA
03 April 2017